THE

Gerard A. Lee is a grad......... .... the
National University of Ir....... .... the
Bar in 1942 he practised c. ... .rn Circuit. A
former lecturer in law at University College, Dublin and at
the Law Society he has contributed many legal and
historical articles to Irish and foreign publications.

Dublin as a European City and other Essays:
Poems

By the same author

A Memoir of the South Western Circuit

GERARD A. LEE, S.C.

Dublin as a European City and other Essays: Poems

WITH A FOREWORD BY

**The Honourable
Mr Justice Declan Costello**

Moytura Press • Dublin

The typesetting of this book was
produced by Gilbert Gough Typesetting for
Moytura Press, Ormond Court,
11 Lower Ormond Quay, Dublin 1.

BRITISH LIBRARY CATALOGUING IN PUBLICATION DATA
Lee, Gerard
Dublin as a European City and other essays: poems
I. Title
941.835

ISBN 1-871305-06-3

Printed in Ireland by
Colour Books Ltd

Contents

Preface   ix

Foreword   xi

Dublin as a European City   1

The Dublin of Jonathan Swift   15

The Beauty of Classical Dublin   37

Along the Liffey Shore   54

Kilfinane and its Setting   76

Some German Cities in 1952   90

The White Knights and their Kinsmen   99

Robert Dwyer Joyce   122

Italian Journey   127

Autumn Leaves— Poetry   133

To the memory of my parents.

Preface

Since boyhood I have been interested in landscape, having spent my early life in a quiet corner of south-east Limerick not far away from the Galtees and the glen of Aherlow. The counties of Cork and Tipperary were near neighbours; our parish was remote from railways or trunk-roads and little change happened or was expected in that great expanse of landscape where the colour and expression of the mountains changed frequently with the seasons or before an approaching storm and where the plains appeared to stretch from the borders of Cork on towards the Rock of Cashel and beyond.

It was a pleasant countryside in which to work and play and to read by the fire, during the long winter evenings, about historic lands as well as tales from the American wilderness. Later, when I practised as a barrister in the south-west, the landscape of parts of Kerry and the unique character of Clare captivated me. After the war it was possible to visit many of the historic places in western Europe and to acquire some little knowledge of the architecture and art, as well as the local history and customs, of those Latins, Franks and Goths who had adorned that great, though turbulent, continent.

In later years I composed the following essays or papers either from personal experience or as a result of research and because of the interest in topography which had been awakened in me during those years of wandering.

These essays do not pretend to be academic or professional; they have been written by an amateur and, while every effort has been made to ensure accuracy, some mistakes of fact are likely to occur. Where they may occur the responsibility is entirely my own.

Acknowledgments

I would like to thank the president and council of the Old Dublin Society for permission to reproduce the essays on the city of Dublin and the essay on the river Liffey all of which had already been published in the *Dublin Historical Record*. I would also like to thank the Rev. editor of *The Furrow* for permission to publish *Italian Journey* which originally appeared in the *Irish Ecclesiastical Record*. Thanks are due to Con Healy, editor of the Limerick Association Yearbook, for permission to reproduce the paper on Kilfinane and to Professor Etienne Rynne for permission to publish the article on the White Knights which first appeared in *North Munster Studies*. The paper on Robert Dwyer Joyce was originally published in the *Irish Independent* in 1948 and many of the poems appeared in *The Kerryman* in the 1960's.

My special thanks are due to Eamonn G. Hall, Solicitor, and to Bart D. Daly, Barrister-at-Law, of the Round Hall Press, for having encouraged me in the publication of this book and to Gerard O'Connor of Moytura Press for having undertaken the task of doing so.

I would like to thank very sincerely the staff in the National Library of Ireland for their help and unfailing courtesy over a long period.

Finally I would like to express my appreciation to the Society of Authors as literary representative of the Estate of James Joyce for permission to reproduce an extract from *Finnegan's Wake*.

Foreword

Gerry Lee has all his life been an enthusiast. As a young man he travelled widely and enthusiastically throughout Europe. Over many years he has, mainly on foot, enthusiastically explored many parts of Ireland and voraciously read history and literature, particularly the history and literature of those parts of Ireland he holds most in affection. He has shared his enthusiasms with his many friends and from time-to-time with a wider audience in the essays he has published. A selection of these is now made available to a new audience. Those who share his interests should welcome the opportunity which is now offered to pursue them in such stimulating company.

The author was born and brought up in south-east Limerick in the small town of Kilfinane close to the borders of Cork and Tipperary. He came to Dublin as a student and has spent a busy and successful life as a barrister on the South Western Circuit and in Dublin. But he has never been a dry-as-dust lawyer, as these essays eloquently testify. His love of his native county, its topography its legends and history has inspired three of them. With considerable scholarship he has traced the history of the White Knights, a Munster branch of the Geraldines. His appreciative essay on the ballads of Robert Dwyer Joyce owes much to a shared appreciation of the beautiful countryside in which they were both brought up and a shared interest in its legends. Robert Dwyer Joyce was born in Glenosheen, which is a few miles from Kilfinane. He became a doctor, a professor of English at the Catholic University, and a prominent Fenian in the United States. It is th poet celebrating the beauty of the Ballyhoura mountains of which the author (with perhaps unconscious self-revelation) writes. His account of Kilfinane itself, its setting and history, is tinged with a little nostalgia. But there is no harm in that. It was a captious critic of Proust who dismissively claimed that other people's nostalgia is boring. Surely this is not so— particularly when, as here, it is conveyed with studied restraint.

The excitment and stimulation of foreign travel are to be found in the author's accounts of his journeys in Germany and Italy. And his love of Dublin, its architecture and history, is that of a native-born Dubliner. He celebrates it here in "Dublin as a European City" and "The Beauty of Classical Dublin" but characteristically he is silent on the depredations of those who have been "developing", and in the process destroying, our capital concentrating instead on what is left to be enjoyed and praised. In a further essay he has skillfully woven an account of Swift's life into a description of Swift's Dublin, enlivening our interest in, and heightening our enjoyment of, both.

O ~~Dublin as a European City~~ may well find a place in future anthologies of modern Irish essays. The author starts it at the Liffey's source high up in the Wicklow mountains and follows the river's course throught the mountains, into the plains of Kildare and through the city. It is obviously a journey with which the author is well familiar. He intimately knows its beauties, its historical and literary associations. He had given much more than a pleasing description of one of Ireland's loveliest rivers—it is a distillation of a lifetimes scholarship and an expression of warm sensibilities.

He ends his account of the Liffey at O'Connell Bridge looking westward over the Dublin skyline towards the splendours of the setting sun. His description hints, as his work elsewhere has hinted, that his sensibilities require a medium other than prose for their complete expression. And so it is no surprise to find a selection of his poetry at the end of this volume. Nor is it a surprise that the idiom he has chosen is that of the romantic poets of the early nineteenth century. By this choice he reaffirms, as he has done throughout all his essays, how the past can triumphantly enrich the present.

DECLAN COSTELLO
The High Court, Dublin 7

Dublin as a European City

Many Dubliners must from time to time have inquired as to how their city can compare with the average city or town of Europe and, indeed, when wandering through the continent, this thought was often uppermost in my mind. The joy which I got at the sight of a beautiful town or building in Spain, Italy or Germany was often chastened by the thought that we had no such glories at home or that, if we had, we would never cease to sing their praises. But in reality have we not got a city which, in its own century and setting, can compare favourably with a similar city in Europe and which contains at least a few churches, a university and some private squares and public parks and buildings which equal and, in some cases, surpass their opposite numbers in the heart of Europe?

With a full appreciation of my limitations in making such a study it is nevertheless a happy task to examine briefly an outline of this comparison and in doing so I will treat the subject from the point of view of architecture, amenities and surroundings.

Architecture: Architecturally Dublin can take a special place in the tradition of European cities. It existed as a settlement in pre-Norse days and, while there is little or nothing left to us as evidence of its importance beyond perhaps a few place-names and the known sites of ancient structures, nevertheless we have in the neighbourhood as in many places throughout the country several ancient pre-Christian and Christian monuments and objects to mark a centre of population or a burial or pilgrimage place of note. An ancient well or a church site or the site of an

1

old graveyard with crosses and rude carvings and lettering sometimes provides tangible evidence of the ancient Christian background of the environs of the city while a dolmen or a cromlech in the hills illustrates the shadowy antiquity of its immediate surroundings.

During the dark ages, which preceded the medieval rebirth of Europe, a great gap appears in the architectural continuity of its cities and its countryside, so much so that, in his essay on the city of Arles, Hilaire Belloc says that, after the fall of Rome, "there came five hundred years of which so little is left in Europe that Paris has but one doubtful tower and London nothing." Yet in the Irish countryside, including the neighbourhood of Dublin, the known presence of churches, monasteries and burial sites, dating from this era, places Ireland as a centre of civilisation and learning while the rich exhibits in the national museum, showing fine craftsmanship in metal and stone, provide evidence of a culture which was vigorous in this country but was, for the time being, eclipsed in the centre of Europe.

Dublin does not claim to be essentially a medieval city in the sense that we spoke in the happier pre-war days of cities like Hildesheim, Nürnberg or Brunswick. These towns were not merely medieval in history and background; their whole appearance and character came from the middle ages. The tall, gabled and gaily painted half-timbered houses, the schloss or burg, the churches and town-hall in the market place and the inevitable winding cobbled streets, red with the glow of geraniums, presented a pattern of a city of the romantic Germany which finds little parallel in Dublin. Dublin could never have been a town of the middle ages in this traditional sense. The warmth and colour necessary to create the atmosphere of the era and to continue it down to the present day could scarcely have existed in our island outpost. In any event the fabric of the medieval streets which once surrounded St. Patrick's and Christchurch has long since vanished and no quaint dwellings or public buildings and no market-place with city hall and fountain exist to stamp an

2

essentially medieval character on the heart of old Dublin. In the place of this, however, we are left with two restored cathedrals, a few churches and fragments of the city wall from these times as evidence of the development and prosperity of Dublin in the centuries before it finally received the character by which it is chiefly known and loved today.

The fact that two cathedrals, belonging to the same religious denomination, survive in the centre of the city must strike many a traveller as unique. This fact is not unique but it is rare and I can recall seeing it occur in only four other cities, namely Salamanca, Saragossa, Coimbra and Brescia. The situation in Dublin, however, differs from all of the others because here both cathedrals are medieval, they have the same architectural style and have existed together through the centuries. In the European examples the medieval cathedral stands by the side of a building erected centuries later and generally for the convenience of a growing city. The older cathedrals of Brescia and Salamanca are Romanesque. They immediately adjoin their more modern counterparts which, in the case of Brescia, is a majestic, although not a very beautiful, Baroque building of the early 17th century while the later cathedral in Salamanca is a glorious example of the blending of Gothic and Baroque. The older buildings in Coimbra and Saragossa also make a striking contrast to the new which, in the latter city, is one of the great religious magnets of Spain — El Pilar. In strong contrast too is the grey stone of our two Irish churches which stands out in relief when compared with the warmer mellow shades of the south.

But how do these old cathedrals of Dublin compare when examined in the light of their average counterpart in Europe? With the exception of the superb churches of Spain, France and Italy I believe they fare well externally while the interior often lacks the rich adornment of the continent. The great artistic wealth of the Latin churches finds little parallel although the simple beauty of the Irish stone-work with its vaulting and its pillars bears a strong comparison with that of the traditional Gothic churches of Europe and is superior in appearance to the often gaunt churches of Holland and Switzerland and some of the sacred buildings of Portugal. But, for all that, one misses here the richness of even the less sumptuous interiors of German cathedrals like Ulm, Bamberg, Freiburg and Regensburg which contain exquisitely-carved objects of late Gothic wood and stone that form such a happy blending with the more sombre walls of the building itself while the characteristic rich medieval stained glass of France is also missing in Dublin.

In this connection it may be of interest to state that many of the famous cathedrals of Germany came through the war without serious destruction although in some cases they stood almost alone like outposts of culture among the ruins of their cities as in Cologne, Ulm, Aachen, Mainz and Freiburg while in some happy instances not merely the cathedrals but also the beautiful old towns came through unscathed as in the case of Speyer, Marburg, Limburg, Bamberg and Regensburg. Noteworthy exceptions occurred in Wurzburg, Minden, Lubeck and Munich where the cathedrals also had been badly damaged or gutted by fire.

A morbid feature of old Dublin can be seen in the church of St. Michan where mummified corpses are preserved apparently by the dry air of the crypt. Like the presence of two medieval cathedrals this too is almost unique but, in the church of St. Francis in Portugal's lovely city of Evora, with it blending of Moorish and European styles, there is a chapel the whole of the walls, pillars and ceilings of which are lined with, or constructed of, skulls and other human bones arranged in symmetrical patterns. The remains of many thousands of human beings are contained in this sombre aisle and were probably arranged in the 17th century and obtained from the contents of ancient crypts.

Europe has many cities which obtain their character from a particular century or style of architecture. With the exception of such museum towns as Pompeii and

Herculaneum the so-called Roman cities of Europe are in reality those with a medieval or more modern character but which contain some noteworthy remains from the days of the Empire. The vast arenas of Verona, Nimes and Arles, the aqueduct of Segovia and the Roman walls of Tarragona are merely interesting and important details which mark the antiquity of the site of the later town. The incursions of the Goths and the Vandals and the long dark age which followed almost obliterated the living towns and it is only since the reign of Charlemagne that we again begin to have living cities some of which survive to the present day. But it is one of the many tragic events of the past generation that so many of the beautiful half-timbered medieval towns should have fallen victim to the fury of the war and, in an era of total war, we have to count ourselves fortunate to be able to point with joy to some of the survivors such as Bruges, Colmar, Goslar and Hamelin as well as to the beautiful picture towns of Bavaria, namely Rothenburg, Dinkelsbühl, Nördlingen and Bamberg.

We must however pass these ages by and come to the 18th and 19th centuries for it was then, in the great days of Georgian and Victorian architecture in these islands that Dublin received the stamp by which we know it today. The fact that the capital received its adornment of clear, classical lines in that earlier century must classify it as essentially an Anglo-Irish rather than an Irish city for that was time when Ireland itself was no better than a nation of beggars before O'Connell became their king and the splendour and glory of Dublin stands in clear contrast to the slow rotting away of the countryside. In strange contrast too to the classical purity of Dublin stands the 18th century style in parts of the continent when fine interiors of many ancient civic and sacred buildings were disfigured by the application of Rococo art with too lavish a hand.

In almost all European cities the hub of life is the great central square. The plazas of Spain, the piazzas of Italy, the platz of Germany and Austria as well as the squares of France and Belgium are not merely social centres of universal popularity, they are also areas for the better display of some of the finest public buildings of the city. The cathedrals or churches very often and the town halls almost invariably are shown to the best advantage by their setting in a splendid open space. In the old principalities of central and southern Europe the Ducal palace is built either in the midst of gardens in the outskirts of the capital or it forms one side of a square if it is situated in the town itself. A fountain or statue usually adorns the square and the remaining sides are often lively with open-air cafes and the sound of music. So important and usual is the open space in the outline of a European city that even the central railway station has its square and many of the everyday commercial and cultural activities take place in the open air in the centre of the town.

The squares of central and suburban Dublin also form an essential feature in the outline of the city. The mansions of the classical squares and the streets which adjoin them give Dublin its most noteworthy quality. It is a Georgian city precisely because of these beautiful areas and of the presence here and there of fine public buildings in the neo-classical style. The warm mellow brick of the houses, with their wine-like colour, provides a welcome for the visitor on a sunlit morning in summer like the glow of lovely Salamanca, rich in its garment of mature sandstone. But the squares of Dublin differ from their counterparts in Europe in one very important manner. They are essentially private. The mansions, often with fine internal decoration and invariably with ornamental doorways, were the property of landlords or influential citizens of English or Anglo-Irish extraction and the central area of the square was railed off as a garden or a lawn for the convenience only of the owners and their families. Even in St. Stephen's Green the presence of railings and the closing of the gates at nightfall betrays this private tendency which finds little parallel on the continent. There, however, the square is invariably paved; it is embellished with statuary and is separate and distinct from the park. In Dublin the squares form a curious

6

mixture of pavement and park, of public highway and semi-private garden. They are a strange blending of the market-place and the home.

The fine public buildings of limestone and granite which adorn the city are essentially in the European tradition. Dublin Castle with its 18th century character, its princely apartments and the lovely Chapel Royal might be compared to the schloss or burg of the former Central European local capitals. It has many a parallel in the Ducal towns of Germany or Italy and the courtyards of the castle are in keeping with the character of an average continental square. Like the Customs House, the Four Courts is externally one of Dublin's most pleasing structures and is superior to any of the legal buildings in Europe. It has none of the heavy appearance of the courthouse in Brussels or in many of the German state capitals and is far more stately than the simple brick courthouse in The Hague. While the Four Courts and the Customs House may have lost much of their old atmosphere internally due to war nevertheless the fine oak interiors of the individual High Courts and the rosewood interior of the Supreme Court, together with the granite pillars and walls of the Round Hall, preserve a traditional atmosphere at least in the main features of the building.

Possibly a unique feature of Dublin is its two universities which, together with King's Inns, the Incorporated Law Society and the Colleges of Surgeons, Science and Veterinary Surgery provide the city with more than the average number of institutions of higher study including the three schools of medicine. King's Inns, where students for the Bar attend their professional as distinct from university lectures and where they keep commons before their call, was designed by Gandon the architect of the Customs House and shows the first imitations of the Greek Revival. With its great dining-hall, its rich and beautiful old library and its atmosphere this building is well worthy of classical Dublin and, like the College of Surgeons which possesses a pleasing facade and beautiful assembly room, it has no exact parallel as an institution on the continent. It finds its basis in the medieval development of the legal profession in England which was followed with little change in Ireland. As a group of university buildings Trinity College gives a stately character to the centre of the city. The great west front, rebuilt in 1752, and the classical architecture and the courtyards are finer than in most of the corresponding institutions in the university towns of the continent. Some of the European foundations are, however, more ancient. In the middle ages Salamanca was numbered with Paris, Bologne and Oxford as one of the four great universities of Europe and it is Salamanca today among the continental towns that still possesses a group of university buildings which, in dignity and beauty, rival those of Trinity College, although the former are built of sandstone which time has mellowed to a warm golden brown whereas the latter possess an attractive blend of limestone and granite.

A feature of the lay-out of Dublin, which contrasts sharply with the average pattern of a continental town, is the presence of large sprawling suburbs. This is a mark of Anglo-Saxon civilisation of which Dublin is the direct social product and in this sense, in proportion to the population of the respective countries, Dublin is a close parallel to London. To a large extent Europeans live in flats and apartments; they live in residential streets rather than residential roads and their playgrounds are the gardens of the public parks and the open-air cafés of the squares. The built-up area of the city is utilised to the utmost and it is rare to find the wasteful use of a site so sadly common in Dublin where much of the centre was formerly wasted with wretched buildings and even shacks and ruined areas. The European town is, accordingly, a more compact and solid unit still retaining to a large extent its medieval outline and, even in the case of large modern capitals like Lisbon or Madrid, the area of the city is nothing like as extensive as that of greater Dublin. A sad feature of this traditional compactness of the continental town was the ease with which many of these centres of culture were destroyed by bombing during the war while the advantages include the presence of a brighter life in the city itself which is not merely a commercial centre but is also a cultural and social centre for the people. The pleasant countryside surrounding the town is largely preserved and, unlike the cruel fate which has fallen on Dublin, those living even in the central streets can get to the amenities of the surrounding woodlands in a short time although in Portugal and Holland there is also a tendency for buildings to spread into the countryside. In the latter case, however, the land has little of the aesthetic value when compared with the surroundings of Dublin and the new building estates are all of brick and are broken here and there with delightful little parks and flower gardens and by the universal Dutch weakness for fine rows of roadside trees. In Dublin a brick and granite city is now surrounded by a wide ring of concrete dwellings often poorly laid out at the expense of the fields and woodlands of former days. In almost all the towns of northern Europe, where the traditional building material is brick, the new housing estates and new structures generally continue to be of brick and in southern Europe, where the warm sunny climate seems to demand and to suit a stucco finish in dwellings, then this traditional method is continued almost always with taste and with the presence of certain features which give personality to the buildings.

Amenities: In dealing with the amenities of Dublin we have proof once again of the Anglo-Saxon character of the city and the amenities to which I refer are those relating to pleasure and pastime. Few cities of its size can have such a large area of space allotted to games. The outskirts abound in playing pitches for hurling, football and rugby and these have invaded even the suburban parks while the golf-courses, which formerly surrounded the suburbs and which in their turn are now surrounded by great areas of housing estates and apartments, have the incidental merit of preserving much of the natural beauty of the landscape. The average continental city has fewer playing pitches although football has a growing popularity in many

European towns. The race-courses, which abound in Ireland, have few parallels on the continent outside some of the larger cities while golf is regarded as a game either solely for foreign tourists or for some of the wealthy citizens of the larger towns or the holiday centres.

Each nation has, of course, its own particular sport. Every large city in Spain and Portugal and in parts of southern France has its bull-ring to which the people throng during the season as they do to the circus or the fun-fair in Ireland and, in winter, the presence of snow in the mountains of Central Europe permits the delightful sport of skiing which can never be more than an idle dream in the mountains of Ireland. The continental game of tennis has also much popularity in Dublin in spite of the moist climate while yachting and boating have a considerable following in the city but this cannot be compared with their popularity abroad. In the holidays and during the week-ends every large and small lake in the Netherlands is white with sails. Every acre of that remarkable little country is used in some way or another and every canal and stream has its boats. The complex of canals in Amsterdam and the other water-towns of Holland, with their launches and boats, are used to their capacity not merely for commerce but for the enjoyment of the citizens.

The beautiful Alster lake, which gives such character to the centre of Hamburg and provides a vast sheet of water in the heart of the town, is one of the most delightful gifts which nature has given to any city and how well have the wise citizens availed of the gift! It is in fact a beautiful playground also white with sails and happy with the shouts of swimmers and bathers in the autumn sunshine like the rivers of the continent as they pass the gray walls of Europe's historic towns. In Germany not merely the cities but even the smaller towns of the Rhine and its lovely tributary streams of the Lahn, the Necker and the Main have their recognised swimming places immediately adjoining and which are brown with the bodies of young bathers organised in their hundreds, while canoes, boats

10

and punts ply hither and thither amidst youthful cheers and which at times gives the character of a South Sea island to these old and well-loved water-towns of Germany.

In every European city the parks play an important role in the social life of the people. They are something more than a centre for recreation. Together with the open-air cafes and squares they are, in fact, the main social centres of the town. In the long summer evenings and at week-ends especially they are lively. People throng to them as in Dublin they go to football matches or on country tours. At a time when Dublin tends to become deserted the continental town becomes filled with people. In Central Europe and in Spain and Portugal, at least in matters of this kind, people are communal as we remain largely individual and it is difficult to find a crowd more homogeneous than that which frequents the ramblas of Spanish and Portuguese towns under the plane-trees before the hour of siesta or in the cool of evening. In smaller provincial cities as in the capital it is everywhere the same and these centres of promenade are as essential a feature of the place as the town-hall or the cathedral itself. It is rather similar in Germany and Austria although the crowds are often smaller and more broken while the playing of music adds to the gaiety of the scene. It is this open-air life of the cities with a background of bands and fountains and with bright cafés and the shade of plane-trees and lindens which is to me of the very essence of civilization. It is one of the elements of European culture and is so much a part of a European's heritage that neither wars nor revolutions have dimmed the dignity and beauty of this most human and refined of all out-door pastimes. In rising again from the ruins of war Hamburg, Bremen and Munich provided these open-air cafes of traditional beauty.

Dublin too has its fine parks. The Phoenix Park is one of the most majestic in Europe. With its rows of oak and chestnuts, its groves of hawthorn and slender birches and the vast spaces, it has few peers but is a little wasted where

11

it lies. It is too far from the main residential areas to be intimate and, with rare exceptions, our civic and social make-up does not allow it to be used as a centre for cultural activities. In cities where the rainfall is almost equal to ours as in Brussels and the Hague and, in Hamburg which lies more northerly, the open spaces are used as well laid-out centres for dancing and music in the summer and autumn evenings. It is in St. Stephen's Green, however, that Dublin has its most European park and very little is needed in order to make it equal to the best of the smaller continental ones. Its beautiful flower beds and fine trees would form a worthy background to a fountain in the Baroque mould placed in the centre of the park where the statue of George II formerly stood. But such a fountain would have to be superb because nothing else is good enough for St. Stephen's Green. At the apex of the fountain I would wish to see a heroic-size statue of the dying Cuchulain — the symbol of our mythical story.

Dublin has its own special amenities which are sometimes not so well developed on the continent. The Royal Dublin Society is one of the finest organisations of its kind which is proved by its many historic, scientific and cultural acitvities and its renowned shows. The Botanic Gardens are certainly among the most beautiful in Europe although they are not visited as frequently as they deserve, while our theatres, though few in number, have a noteworthy tradition. Indeed the city itself is a centre for lovers of literature and what single town in Europe, with some exceptions, can compare with Dublin as a city of literary men since the days when Swift wrote his Gulliver's Travels!

Surroundings: Few cities can compare with Dublin in the beauty of its environs. If nature gave the lovely Alster lake to the heart of Hamburg and if she provided Innsbruck with a range of mountains of incomparable majesty the superb bay of Dublin and the ranges of heather hills which stretch far to the south illustrate some of the gifts which she has given to us with a lavish hand. Among the towns

12

of Central Europe which justly boast of their surroundings are Stuttgart, Freiburg, Baden-Baden, Innsbruck, Salzburg and Heidelberg. Well may they proudly acclaim their beauty for the wooded mountains and often vine-clad hills which surround or adjoin these old cities have all the attractions which we associate with the German and Austrian highlands. As in almost every other civic detail a contrast must however be made between the European and the Irish. These woodland cities of Central Europe are in their essence civilized and refined. The glory of Dublin's mountain heritage, on the other hand, lied in its wildness. A walk in the Odenwald above Heidelberg is much more like an afternoon stroll when compared to a walk over the Three Rock mountain into Enniskerry. A mountain railway takes you from the town to the hilltop in a few minutes and, if you then feel like it, an open-air café provides refreshments at this early stage. The paths along which you go are carefully marked and the abundant forest provides a welcome shade or shelter with the changing seasons. In Freiburg or Baden-Baden possibly a greater variety is provided by their proximity to the Black Forest but all of these woodland walks, beautiful as they undoubtedly are, have an air of monotony because of the very wealth of the forest and the comparative absence of changing colours so familiar to the Irish scene.

Some of the chief attractions of Dublin and Wicklow mountains, on the other hand, lie in the blending of heather and moorland and the presence of mountain streams and lakes. Should the weather be reasonably clear the view from the top is often splendid and to come back to a good Dublin meal after a day's tramping in the hills is to enjoy some of the greatest pleasures which the city can offer. Each particular walk has its own special attractions such endless variety is there in the environs of the city. Not far from Rathfarnham are the wooded roads at Rockbrook, Willbrook and Marley with an easy ascent of Kilmashogue, Tibradden or the Two and Three Rock mountains and the descent by the Glencullen valley and the Cookstown river into Enniskerry. A pleasant seaside walk includes the Hill of Howth or the cliff path from Bray to Greystones while a short stroll along the waterworks at Bohernabreena can have few rivals for colour and charm in spring or in one of the mature days of autumn.

To those who seek harder ground the climb of Kippure by the two Loughs Bray or the climb of Tonelagee from the base near Lough Nahanagan is very rewarding especially if, in the latter case, you picnic on the descent by the shore of lovely Lough Ouler hidden away in the folds of some of the foothills. Likewise the beautiful glacier valley which connects Loughs Tay and Dan adjoins some of the wildest mountain districts of Wicklow for not far across country is Mullaghcleevaun in the centre of many of the lesser mountains and overlooking the vast reservoir of Pollaphuca.

This is our heritage — a Georgian and Victorian city with many flaws and blemishes but with an ancient background and a vigorous literary and artistic tradition. It is a city in a European island but not of Europe in the full meaning of that term. While, in general outline, it may compare with its average counterpart on the continent neverthless the details of difference due to climate, history and race are so many and so various that Dublin, in its lovely setting of hills and the sea and with its essential Anglo-Saxon character but with a growing international flavour, may justly be proud of its individuality. In conclusion I think it is not unkind to say that, while one-third of Dublin is ugly and another third is commonplace, yet the remaining third is very beautiful and worthy of the charm and dignity of a European capital.

The Dublin of Jonathan Swift

One of the most attractive aspects of the old city Dublin is
the silhouette of the towers and spires of the medieval town
on the south bank when seen against a pale-blue sky
streaked by the red clouds of a late-winter sunset—Christ
Church, St. Audoen's, the Church of SS.Augustine and
John the Baptist and the lovely copper dome of Adam and
Eve's while, not far away, rises the graceful spire of St.
Patrick's crowning its ancient tower and the great
cathedral bulk. On the other side of the Liffey stand the
Norman-style tower of St. Michan's and the exquisite
classical facade and green dome of Arran Quay. When seen
from Grattan bridge, or along the river bank, they form
one of the finest clustered groups of buildings in Europe
and similar in tone to the heart of medieval Ghent.

As we proceed southwards to the area of St.Patrick's
Close with its ancient cathedral, the early 18th century
Marsh's library, the great gaunt deanery and the site of
the former palace of the archbishops, it is there that the
ghost of Swift seems always to linger when the fog and
gloom of early winter have settled on this old corner of the
city near the river.

Great artists are for ever associated with the places of
their birth or creative genius. We remember Avignon and
Vaucluse partly because of Petrarch, while we associate
Florence and Ravenna with Dante. Many literary pil-
grimages are made to Weimar, Wetzlar and Frankfurt-
on-the-Main because of the memories of Goethe and, if
properly presented, Dublin could become a traditional
literary shrine for Ireland's creative writers, because it is
here in Dublin that literature received some of its most

15

expressive and permanent forms, starting with the rather harsh satire of Swift and continuing with the correlated tone and mood of O'Casey and Joyce, of Behan and Flan O'Brien. Like many other old capital cities, Dublin has a particular personality, a very special type of character, and a sense of humour all of its very own. It is racy of the soil, it is cynical and it came largely from that strange accident of history which caused Dublin, the second city of a large empire, to be situated in the territory of a subdued race. How fortunate we are however that so many buildings and personal objects closely associated with Swift and his circle have survived for our literary benefit and delight in the centre and surroundings of the city!

DUBLIN AFTER THE RESTORATION

When the Duke of Ormond returned to Dublin, as Viceroy, in 1662, the Middle Ages ended at last and only then did Dublin become a capital in any modern sense. At the Restoration the city was about one ninth of a square mile in extent. Like London it was a rectangle with one of the larger sides bordering the river and crossed by a single bridge to the Norse suburb of Oxmanstown. In the southeast corner, the castle corresponded to the Tower of London and in the centre stood Christ Church Cathedral in a semi-ruinous condition.[1] Little remains now of the actual fabric of the medieval city although the castle, the cathedrals and some of the old churches, happily, have remained, in a restored or altered form mostly, on, or near, the hill around Christchurch Place in the ancient heart of the city as tangible proof of the strange foreign origin and continuity of Ireland's capital.

To the south, around St. Patrick's Cathedral, was the old Irish quarter in the valley of the Poddle, well equipped with churches dedicated to Irish saints. East of the town, on a little hillock by the sea, were the Elizabethan buildings of Trinity College, near the ancient Norse Thingmote and the Long Stone[2] which stood adjacent to

16

the medieval leper hospital of St. James where the Steyne river flowed into the Liffey in the vicinity of the present Townsend Street. Gradually the space between the castle and the college became a long street and, near its eastern end, the Round Church was built as a successor to the early church of St. Andrew which originally stood in Dame Street close to the gate of the Lower Castle yard, and as a predecessor of the present fine church in Suffolk Street.

Oxmanstown (the town of the Ostmen) expanded to become a residential district with fine houses around its Green. Soon more bridges were built and ships berthed only below the castle gate. Over the meadows south-east of the city new streets began to stretch, much wider and straighter, which culminated in a grand square of twenty-seven acres, two sides of which were built over by 1685.[3] This was St. Stephen's Green named after the late-medieval leper-house of St. Stephen which stood on the site of the former Mercer's Hospital and traditionally dedicated to the first martyr like the lazar-houses of Cork and Waterford. Oxmanstown Green was, unfortunately, built on to a large extent with Queen Street as the highway and Smithfield as the market place.[4] In Queen Street itself a modest collegiate building — the Blue Coat School or Hospital of King Charles — was being erected and of which Swift later became a governor. This building was superseded in 1777 by Thomas Ivory's magnificent edifice which stands today in Blackhall Place.

Beyond it all lay the vast green meadows of the Phoenix Park which commenced as a royal deer park in 1662 and which, by 1680, had attained its present extent and its potential as probably the largest and most beautiful urban park in the world. In the latter year also, on the ruins of the Priory of the Knights Hospitallers of St. John at Kilmainham, a large quadrangular building with an internal arcade was arising in the form of the Royal Hospital designed by Sir William Robinson. What a happy thought, amidst so much confusion and ugliness, to find that the Castle and the Royal Hospital have today been carefully restored!

It was into this growing city of the Restoration that Jonathan Swift was born, probably in Hoey's Court, on the feast of St. Andrew 1667 and, on his death in 1745, the development of the later and splendid city of Georgian and neo-classical art had well started upon its way. Essex bridge was completed in 1678 and became the focal point of Dublin for 100 years. Capel Street, Jervis Street and Ormond Quay were laid out; the slender line of quays was commenced and remains a feature of great potential beauty when the river is at full tide and slowly reaching for the sea under its graceful stone bridges, with the view unimpeded towards the west and made lovely on the evening of a clear sunset. The government of Ormond and his successors planned and laid out this fine patrician city. The disgrace will be ours if we further mar the fabric of what is still one of the most authentic period cities of the world.

It is now time to consider the intellectual and literary background of the Dublin into which Swift was born. Earlier Dublin writers existed but they had little organic relation to Irish life. Perhaps the most deserving of our gratitude and respect is Sir James Ware who published Latin treatises on Irish ecclesiastical and literary antiquities. He collected Irish manuscripts, and his great service to the country was the publication of his *Irish Writers* in 1639 and *Irish Antiquities* in 1654 which entitled him to an honoured place among those who were dedicated to rescue the monuments of Gaelic Ireland from oblivion.[5] About that time also Dr. Gerard Boate compiled *The Natural History of Ireland* and William Petty prepared the *Down Survey* and later wrote *The Political Anatomy of Ireland*. Of the famous Molyneux brothers, who were fourth generation settlers in Ireland, it was William who published in 1698 the well-known tract *The Case of Ireland Stated* which stands first in the succession later to be followed by the *Drapier's Letters* in asserting Ireland's legislative independence on grounds unconnected with race or any separate allegiance. Like the latter, it was evoked by a particular act of British policy towards Ireland in the form of a series of laws aimed at the destruction of the Irish wool trade. It was left to Jonathan Swift however to break new ground and to present his genius in the form of creative writing and thereby establish that particular form of art in Dublin for which Ireland has since been famous in a proportion far in excess of its size and far greater, too, than its fame in the visual arts of painting and sculpture.

SWIFT AS VICAR AND DEAN

Swift was probably born in a tall Jacobean house in Hoey's Court, which was the home of his uncle Godwin. Conservative opinion believes that his father was Jonathan Swift who held the humble post of steward of King's Inn. The future dean, they hold, was a posthumous son whose father died after a brief married life leaving a widow and possibly two other children.

It matters little for the purpose of the present essay whether the future dean was the son of this humble steward or was the natural child of Sir John Temple, the Master of the Rolls, or whether Stella was the natural child of the judge's son, Sir William Temple, as Denis Johnston has submitted in a brilliant argument.[6] Neither does it matter whether Swift was secretly married to Stella in the grounds of the deanery, or whether the younger and more passionate Vanessa was his mistress. These fine elements of detective work belong to a smaller, but infinitely more detailed, canvas than the scope of the present paper. Among the many biographers of Swift — and they have never been impartial — two, whose views are the least reconcilable, are Denis Johnston and Dr. Wyse Jackson. The former presents Swift as a normal full-blooded man caught by a series of dilemmas and frustrations which kindled his wrath into savage irony, and the latter paints a picture of simplicity in which everything operates to show the faithful Dean of St. Patrick's as a model of ecclesiastical virtue. The contrast between the two accounts varies in almost direct ratio to the interpretation put on *Gulliver's Travels* as an essay of savage indignation (which it is), or as a story for the amusement of children (which it also is). One of the fascinations of Swift is that he was, and remains, a perpetual puzzle for most of those who try to explain the actions and the writings of that strange, volatile, depressive personality.

When Swift had passed through Kilkenny College and had received his degree at Trinity he became secretary to Sir William Temple at Moor Park in Surrey and it was there that he became acquainted with Esther Johnson known to the world for ever as Stella. In 1694, Swift was ordained deacon and provided with the tiny prebend of Kilroot in the Diocese of Connor. After eighteen months on the shores of Belfast Lough he returned to Moor Park but not until a love affair with Varina involved him to the point of a proposal which was apparently rejected, but whose later advances annoyed him to the point of a reply in which, he put the truth in the most naked words and turned them loose upon Varina. It is a letter worth reading as the wording of it was like a trial-run for his later magnetic masterpieces. Swift continued at Moor Park from 1696 until Sir William Temple's death in 1699 during which time *A Tale of a Tub* was completed and the *Battle of the Books* composed. He became Temple's close and esteemed counsellor and friend; he was tutor to Stella, and he wrote a few Pindaric odes which caused Dryden to say: "Cousin Swift, you will never be a poet", but for which Dryden, in his turn, was later made to look ridiculous by Swift in his encounter with Virgil in the battle of the books. After Temple's death Swift faithfully edited and arranged the publication of his old patron's posthumous works. The presentation copy of Temple's *Letters to the King* is preserved in Marsh's library which was erected about the year 1700 by the archbishop on the grounds of the ancient palace to the east of St. Patrick's Cathedral. The *Letters* contain Swift's own name on the title page as publisher and, on the fly leaf, they have been inscribed "To His Grace, Narcissus, Lord Primate of all Ireland". At a later date

Swift penned a most uncharitable character of Marsh but, at this time, the archbishop was his patron having presented Swift with the prebend of Dunlavin in St. Patrick's Cathedral.

In 1700 Swift obtained the rectory of Agher and vicarages of Laracor and Rathbeggan all in the diocese of Meath. Laracor, situated not far from Trim, was the principal parish of the union. The old church of the parish has long since disappeared and the present solid stone building was erected about 1860. Today it stands near the cross-roads surrounded by its graveyard and some splendid beech and chestnut trees in that rich rolling country of Meath on the edge of the great plains. On the other side of the road nearby is the site of the old vicarage and garden of the early 18th century, with the Kinghtsbrook river flowing past under the stone bridge, and, in the neighbourhood may still be seen some of the mansions embosomed in their beech woods.

A picture of the former church at Laracor still exists and there are traditional descriptions of its interior. The community of Laracor was a tiny one. In a *Visitation of the Diocese* made in 1723 it is reported that, while there were but few Protestant families in the parish, some of them were very wealthy. A handsome classical tablet stood in the old church which gave an appreciation of the services of Garret Wesley to church and state and this tablet now decorates the present building. Sometimes Stella and her chaperon Mrs. Dingley, came to hear Swift preach in his church, and, on these visits, they are believed to have stayed in a cottage near Trim. Even when he became the Dean of St. Patrick's, Laracor continued to be held by Swift until his death in 1745. He spent much of his time there and loved the quiet homeliness of the place. He improved the vicar's house and the garden; he dammed the stream and made a walled fish-pond and, beside the stream and under the willows, he made a little walk.[7] As Vaucluse was to Petrarch, so was Laracor to Swift. It soothed and refreshed him. Fleeing from the pains of unrequited love, Petrarch sought refuge from Avignon in the Closed Valley

21

where, expressing his lovely Latin thoughts, he said: "In this desperate pass, I perceived a rock upon a secret shore, a refuge against disaster. And now, hidden among the hills, I weep my past life". There Petrarch went, and he would yet write canzoniere which would astonish the world. In a letter to his friend, Giovanni Colonna, the poet said: "You will see me content with a small but shady garden and a tiny house, which will seem all the tinier on receiving so great a guest. You will see me from morn to eve wandering alone among the meadows, hills, springs and woods. I flee men's traces, love the shadows, enjoy the mossy caves and the greening fields, curse the cares of the Curia, avoid the city's tumult, refuse to cross the thresholds of the mighty, mock the concerns of the mob. I am equidistant from joy and sadness, at peace by day and night. I glory in the Muses' company, in bird-song and the murmur of water-nymphs. My servants are few but my books are many . . .".[8] How similar is the emotion of Swift when, during his commission in London to secure the grant of the First Fruits from the Government, he pines for Laracor and, in a letter to Stella, dated the 19th march 1711, he cries: "O that we were at Laracor this fine day! The willows begin to peep and the quicks to bud. My dream is out; I was a dreaming last night that I ate ripe cherries. And now they begin to catch the pikes and will shortly the trouts, and I would fain know whether the floods were ever so high as to get over the Holly bank or the river walk; if so, then all my pikes are gone, but I hope not".[9] And when he had lived in the big rambling deanery at St. Patrick's, he fled for solace to Laracor: "I prefer a field-bed and an earthen floor", he said, "before the great house they say is mine". It was in June 1713 that Swift was installed in Dublin as Dean of a massive and dilapidated Gothic Cathedral, master of a gloomy and rambling deanery, and ruler of an independent neighbourhood called the Liberty of the Dean of St. Patrick's. He was then 46 years old, and "Lord Mayor of one hundred and twenty houses".

MEMORIES OF THE DEAN IN DUBLIN

One of the more fortunate events in the history of Dublin, from the literary point of view, is that so many of the places associated with Swift have come down to modern times with little serious alteration, or loss of association, in the course of more than two centuries. A similar happy result has attended the history of much of the personal property and objects connected with him. St. Patrick's has, of course, been restored but it remains very like the cathedral which he governed for thirty-two years. The present granite spire was not erected until 1749 and some of the monuments and decorations are of later vintage. Plenty of stained glass decorates the windows, and it is then, when the sunlight is streaming through, casting its glow on, or around, the graves of Swift and Stella, or when the late autumn fog descends on the old-world streets and the cathedral close nearby, that I like to wander slowly through this vast church, gazing on the monuments and at peace in an atmosphere of colour and quiet, broken sometimes by the music of a Bach cantata from the organ.

The small, rather charming, memorial which Swift erected in 1722 to his servant Alexander McGee, still remains. It was placed there "in memory of McGee's discretion, fidelity and diligence in that humble station". The more recent memorial to Carolan, the last of the bards, stands almost opposite the vast baroque monument of Richard Boyle. There too is the fierce epitaph of Swift and one of Stella, and the fine marble bust of the dean presented by Faulkner, his printer and publisher. But it is the small brass plates on the floor which are the most moving of all the monuments. These cover the graves of the two persons whose friendship was one of the strangest and, apparently, one of the most sincere, but mysterious, in all the history of literature. Their bones still lie side by side — those of Swift and Stella — and the writing simply records their names and the dates of their respective deaths. In the cathedral also are preserved Swift's pulpit, formerly on wheels, the semi-circular communion table from Laracor and some books.

Between the cathedral and the site of the old palace of the archbishops, which is now a police station, is the charming brick and limestone building of Marsh's library with its attractive shape and completely old-world interior, full of atmosphere, which can have changed but little since Swift was there as a reader and a governor in the early 18th century. The marginal notes of the dean, written in the 1707 edition of Clarendon's *History of the Rebellion and Civil Wars in England,* have always been an object of interest to visitors. In the whole series of marginal jottings it is quite a relief to find occasionally one that varies the virulence of the writer's hatred of Scotland and the Scots. In some of the marginal notes Swift criticises, or corrects, Clarendon's English. These are especially interesting as expressing the views of a master of simple and lucid prose. Similarly, in the Blue-Coat School, of which Swift was also a governor, a momento of the dean existed in the form of a portrait which hung in the lobby above the fine main staircase of the school when it was in Blackhall Place and not in Queen Street as in the days of the dean. Another fine bust of Swift may be seen in the library of Trinity College. This was made by the French sculptor, Louis Francois Roubiliac and has a very sinsitive treatment of the subject's face. It was presented by the fourth year students to the library where an exhibition was held in 1945 to commemorate the bicentenary of the death of the dean. Many of the items were lent by institutions or private owners. Several early editions of Swift's works and books relating to him as well as manuscripts, portraits and personal relics were on view.

Apart from the early editions of books, the most interesting relics were Roubiliac's bust, a portrait in oils by Charles Jervas, another portrait by an unknown artist which is now in the Provost's House, a death-mask which was cast from the original and is now in the School of Anatomy in Trinity, miniatures of Swift and Stella, an engraving of Vanessa, a water-colour sketch of the ruins of the vicarage at Laracor; and, lastly, an oblong snuff-box of the dean's inscribed on the inside of the lid with eight lines of verse. Among the treasures in Trinity College library is a fragment of autobiography called the *Autofrag* which is written in Swift's own hand in the third person and covers the first thirty years of his life.

On the side of St. Patrick's Close opposite the cathedral and Marsh's library stands the Deanery House which occupies the original site. Here Swift lived and wrote between 1713 and 1745. Although much of the interior was destroyed by a fire in 1781, the exterior remains much the same and, together with Mansion House and the Provost's House, the deanery of St. Patrick's continues as one of the old mansions of Dublin still used, in effect, for its original private or semi-private purpose. Among the portraits of deans one of the most interesting is that of Swift painted by Bindon in 1739 at the expense of the chapter. The Liberty of the Dean of St. Patrick's which occupied the surrounding streets was an area of five and a half acres and, in olden days, it had the privilege of sanctuary and its own court and gaol. By survival from the original Anglo-Norman foundation, the dean had rights and duties as a magistrate.

But, of all the buildings associated with the dean, perhaps the one most poignantly personal is St. Patrick's Hospital which was built from the design of George Semple, in 1749, following the bequest in Swift's will. As far back as November 1731, when he wrote his own *Verses on the Death of Dr. Swift*, the scheme had been formed for the concluding quatrain consists of the celebrated jest:

> He gave the little Wealth he had,
> To build a House for fools and mad:
> And shewed by one satyric Touch,
> No Nation wanted it so much.

Today, with the exception of valuable extensions and up-to-date equipment, most of what is finest in the original 18th century building has been carefully, and even lovingly preserved. The fine facade of Dublin granite with its classical lines and carved inscription is still the same. On ascending the original curved stone stairway are stained-glass windows depicting the coat of arms of the dean, and of Robert Emmet, father of the patriot. A small museum has been started in the beautiful boardroom with its Adam's mantel-piece, its panelled walls and the portraits of Swift, Stella and Vanessa. The dean's writing desk, with its secret drawers and wallnut fittings, is preserved there and a triangular silver snuff-box which belonged to him. Swift's watch, which is probably Genevan of late 17th century design, is also preserved in the little museum. It has dials to show the day of the month and the phases of the moon. Several other historic items are collected including the book of specifications and plans for St. Patrick's Hospital by George Semple, the bills for Swift's coffin and funeral and four portraits of the dean. Two other momentos of him consist of an engraving, cut in paper in black and white, by Nathaniel of Dublin from *circa* the year 1760, which is preserved in the Civic Museum in William Street, and a plaque on the pillar of a gateway in Little Ship Street stating that, in No.7 Hoey's Court, about 100 feet north west of the spot, it is reputed that Swift was born.

At an early age Swift proved himself to be a man of independence and of courage. By the publication of *A Tale of a Tub*, he mortally offended important members of the Church of England and so put beyond his reach an English bishopric to which he aspired, and which might have given him status and social prestige to satisfy his ambition and soothe his temperament. But, once his talent had been launched on the stormy seas of satire and irony, he guided his ship with fortitude through these seas with the publication of *Gulliver*, the *Drapier's Letters*, and the shocking, though facetious *Modest Proposal*. It was with bravery, too, that he faced and endured, throughout the greater part of his life, the recurrent depressions with the resulting mental anguish and savage indignation to which his sensitive and highly nervous temperament was a victim.

Swift, too, was proud and vain but he had the just ambition of a man of intellect and genius. His relationship with Sir William Temple and Archbishop King often smarted more of vanity than humility or respect, while Dryden's disparaging remark on his poetic powers may have led to a life-long hostility. His cold haughtiness to the highest in the land was not only recognised but universally feared. Swift, the denouncer of pride as the cardinal sin, yet said to Pope on one occasion: "I am so proud, I make all the great Lords come up to me", which inspired Pope to write his well-known lines:

'Yes, I am proud; I must be proud to see
Men not afraid of God afraid of me;
Safe from the Bar, the Pulpit and the Throne
Yet touched and shamed by ridicule alone'.

A very human ambition of his was to be popular and successful in society. His success in political and social life in England after the publication of *The Tale* must have made these years amongst the happiest in his life and the role of an English ambassador, bishop or minister of state would have given him the forum and the company which he sought. Like all literary men he had the ambition to become a poet, for poetry expresses the true art of literature, and, when he failed, he turned his fury against the inhabitants of Grub-street with words of magnificent scorn:

"Not Beggar's Brat, on bulk begot;
Nor Bastard of a Pedlar Scot;
Nor Boy brough up to cleaning Shoes,
The Spawn of *Bridewell*, or the Stews;
Nor infants dropt, the spurious Pledges
of Gipsies littering under hedges,
Are so disqualified by Fate
To rise in *Church*, or*Law*, or *State*,
As he, whom Phebus in his Ire
Hath *blasted* with poetick Fire."

He carried through, however, his greatest and most praiseworthy ambition by expressing for posterity his unique genius in the form of his famous essays. These were not written for pastime. They saw the burning of much midnight oil at their birth.

If Swift had malice in his pen, perhaps it may be more truly said that this malice was blended with idealism rather than standing alone in scorn and ridicule. In the verses which he wrote on himself he airily said:

"Yet Malice never was his Aim;
He lashed the Vice but spared the name;
No Individual could resent,
Where Thousands equally were meant."

The mixture of his satire, malice and idealism had, as its object, the correction and reform of fallen man, but he did it without love. His genius and his compassion clashed, and the resulting flow of biting satire produced his masterpieces, but failed to win reform.

His most *enduring* quality as a man was his genuine hatred of injustice and tyranny and his defence of its victims whether as Drapier or dean. This basic nobility of his manhood found positive scope in his personal charity towards the poor and in the ultimate establishment of St. Patrick's Hospital for the mentally ill. But his most *endearing* quality was the nature of his friendships. His long conversations with Addison in early life; his unbroken friendship with Gay and Arbuthnot, with Bolingbroke and Pope[10] but, above all, his most human, most touching and most understandable friendship with, or affection for, both Stella and Vanessa have won for him a lasting place among the affections, or criticisms, of men and women who understand the language both of literature and of love.

When young Jonathan was tutor to Stella at Moor Park and, later, while vicar at Laracor, the relationship between them was always the same. They spent quiet days together in the garden at Laracor while Stella and Mrs. Dingley probably lived in the little cottage down the road towards

Trim. It is not difficult to understand that happiness which each gave to the other and the comfort and consolation which Stella was to the dean during the periods of his great creative energy, as hostess at the deanery or in the agonies of his depressive illness, while his letters to her from England which comprise the *Journal to Stella* perpetuate the tone of their affection and provide much of the information which we have about Esther Johnson.

Vanessa's father came originally from Amsterdam and was attainted by the Patriot Parliament before the battle of the Boyne. Having later joined Schomberg's camp at Lisburn, he sat for Derry city in the Williamite Parliament and became Lord Mayor of Dublin in 1697. He was buried in St. Andrew's Church in 1704. Vanessa was born in 1688 and died in 1723. Like her father, she was buried under the floor of the old Round Church of St. Andrew's, but the place where her remains now lie, in relation to the present church, cannot be found.

About the year 1714, Vanessa (Esther Vanhomrigh) came to live at Marlay Abbey in Celbridge which had been the property of her father and, until her death nine years later, both women lived within a few miles of each other and of the dean now installed in his cathedral. There are still nostalgic memories at Celbridge. The Abbey is much the same today — just a little more wind-swept and the great trees in the garden even more splendid. The giant beech and chestnuts spread themselves over the Liffey, which flows through the grounds under the beautiful old bridle-bridge, and over the mill-race which runs like a canal near the rhododendron path and by the cloistered columns of the great yew trees. As a symbol of our story there is Vanessa's bower, a small semi-circular stone seat facing the weir, where the waters of the river divide and where, local legend fondly insists, Vanessa and the dean met and talked.

Jonathan Swift was born to the misfortune of personal insecurity. Either a posthumous or a natural child, have it as you will, he never knew paternal affection and guidance while his relations with his mother, whom he obviously loved, were often severed by his living and study in Ireland. The tardiness of recognition and office taught him the fickleness of success with the resulting fear of poverty and the frustration of disappointed ambition. This insecurity, his attacks of giddiness and deafness and the fears of possible insanity sometimes haunted him as a result of these periods of melancholy and despondency to which he was subject and which, in their turn, were often accelerated by the pressure of those fears. Add to these the daily round, the tattle, and the gossip of a sounding-board like Dublin to a system so nervous, a temper so irritable, a mind so active and it all hastened the end from which he was so often in headlong flight. In the last four years, when fate caught up with him, he presented a tragic picture pacing up and down through the rooms of his gloomy home, or picking a morsel of food alone, without the company of friends, the comfort of Stella, or the consolation of further creative writing.

On his appointment as dean he had said: "I was at first horribly melancholy but it began to wear off and change to dullness". The disagreements with his chapter, the loss of companionship and the stirring scenes in London which he had recently left all tended to produce discontent and acted injuriously on his despondent imagination. Literature, politics, and the society of friends dispelled for a while this melancholy for Swift was a gregarious, but insecure, person to whom loneliness was often akin to despair in a land that, for him, was banishment and among a people whom he understood but little and respected less. In a letter to Pope, written in 1731, he said: "My poetical fountain is drained and I profess I grow gradually so dry that a rhyme with me is almost as hard to find as a guinea and even prose speculations tire me almost as much". His greatest burden, he felt, was not his years but his infirmities and, in the fullness of his life, at the age of seventy-eight, they buried him in his cathedral not far from the remains of the only person for whom he ever felt the warmth of mature affectionate love.

The question may now be asked; on what basis have the

supporters of Swift the right to claim for their champion the character of an Irish patriot? The answer simply is, none. The disruption of the national spirit which commenced with Henry VIII and continued through the reigns of Elizabeth and James I, through the protectorate of Cromwell and the Houses of Orange and Hanover excludes the possibility of any patriot supporting or taking office under these regimes. The dissolution of the monastic foundations and the Knights Hospitaller, the tragic Desmond rebellion and nine years war, the plantations and the final defeat at Aughrim and Limerick followed by the penal laws and cruel social and political tyranny of the early 18th century were all the products of those regimes. When the leaders left for Europe with the flight of the Earls and, later, with the 'Wild Geese' a fundamental element in the distinctive national and cultural existence was lost for ever. The old aristocratic Ireland had been defeated and it was only under O'Connell that a new and more democratic one commenced its tortuous birth. Meanwhile, some element of that spirit was kept alive through the beautiful, though sad, *aisling* or love songs of the poets of the Maigue and of Slieve Luachra or by the memories of Landen or Fontenoy during the awful rotting away of the 18th century when the country was left desolate and without a leader.

What did Swift think of it all? In the first place he held office under the Hanoverians. He largely despised the Irish whom he did not understand while their ideals were ridiculed by him. In his travels through Ireland it is true that he bemoaned the state of the country and the misery of its people. He defended the people directly in the *Drapier's Letters* and obliquely in the *Modest Proposal* but it was done by one who hated oppression and tyranny and he made it quiet clear that he stood first for the king whom he regarded as the legitimate ruler of both Ireland and England. And Swift, who never offended the principle of strict intellectual honesty and integrity, explained to Pope: "I do profess, without affectation", he said, "that your kind opinion of me as a patriot is what I do not deserve; because what I do is owing to perfect rage and resentment and the mortifying sight of slavery, folly and baseness about me, among which I am forced to live". On the constitutional question of the penal laws he had nothing to say and, in reply to Chevalier Wogan, one of the most romantic of the 'Wild Geese', who raised this question, he replies diplomatically: "I cannot but highly esteem those gentlemen of Ireland who, with all the disadvantages of exiles and strangers have been able to distinguish themselves by their valour and conduct in so many parts of Europe, I think, above all other nations".

A man who was among the most luminous thinkers in English literature could not appreciate the cultural and emotional beauty of Irish patriotic feeling. He was not prepared to write or speak, let alone to die, for such an ideal of whose emotional disturbance he was singularly innocent. In a lifetime Swift could not have written what Mangan wrote in a day:

> 'The judgement hour must first be nigh
> Ere you can fade, ere you can die
> My dark Rosaleen'.

The dean could not be expected to understand the nostalgic longing and loneliness which the poet expressed in *Mo Roisin Dubh*.

SWIFT AS A CREATIVE WRITER

Swift always claimed to have used language which could be understood by every literate person but he succeeded so well in hiding a wealth of meaning in his pure lucid prose that academic critics still argue over the meaning of his words. The dualism of *Gulliver's Travels* is known to everyone but it is the humour in *Gulliver* which has given it a place among the famous books of the world and invevitably resulted in its becoming a popular story-book

32

for children who are always highly amused, and not horrified, by the last episode.[11]

It is in this humour and in the brilliant use of wit, ridicule and irony, coupled with his favourite device of parody, in the writing of a popular book of travels, that we find the hall-mark of Swift's creative genius. The hidden but savage indignation behind his silken lash penetrates into the reality of things exposing the lazar-sores of society with its shams and pretence. It is the terrible earnestness and passion of the man which frightens but, when directed against the establishment, and not against its victims, by a clerk in Holy Orders for whom much was at stake and who was often wretchedly ill, we also have the real measure of Swift's courage.

Occasionally he was malicious and unkind by attacking an individual enemy but, for the greater part, he blended humour and cynicism into satire which he described as "a sort of glass wherein beholders do generally discover everybody's face but their own". With this oblique approach the satirical writings of the dean have a power of fascination and stand on a high plane among the masterpieces of creative writing. Swift needs no *apologia* today either as a man or as an artist. His image, his voice, and his art have become part of Dublin's heritage. The earlier Dublin writers were largely scholars and pioneers in historic and scientific research. Swift was the first Dubliner who wrote in a creative literary medium. In one of his essays on Swift's satire (1964), Herbert Davis states that the real object of the *Tale of a Tub* was to ridicule the corruption which the author saw in English letters during the latter half of the 17th century, destroying what he felt had been its finest achievements. This belief was repeatedly stated, and never modified, the standards of good taste in English being a simplicity which was unaffected by fashion, such as he found in the writings of the Elizabethans.[12] Swift can indeed be proudly claimed today as the father of Anglo-Irish literature and, perhaps, the most original writer in the English language.

He was often regarded as an exile in Ireland. He held

office under Ireland's enemies and thereby forfeited the right ever to be claimed as a patriot. But, when in office, he defended an unfortunate people against the establishment and thereby, whatever his motives may have been, he has merited our love. Swift was, in many ways, a rather typical citizen of the Anglo-Irish colonial city which never was, either in its origins or its development, an Irish city but had a character parallel to one of the free cities of the Baltic whose spiritual home lay beyond the seas and with little allegiance to the hinterland. He was a Dubliner with a rather puritanical approach to life and letters and he lashed the pretence which he found in both. The magnitude of his scorn was saved from the charge of cruelty by the exquisite *finessé* of his argument, the classical purity and conciseness of his prose style and by the many sturdy shoulders which were the object of his attack and which, in their numbers, were well able to take the sting. In this he has created the medium of Dublin's literary expression. Satire, ridicule and irony allow full play for the more masculine forms of wit and humour but they are rarely accompanied by gentleness, sentiment, aesthetic feeling or lyrical expression with its deep and varied colours. And this, for good or ill, has been the mood of the later Dublin writers. What Swift was to the 18th century city, in its particular background and time, O'Casey, Shaw and Joyce were to the early 20th century. Their voice is often as harsh as his, though their audience is nearer to the soil. When Shaw was asked why he did not write a book on Swift, he replied that he was too busy carrying on his work.[13] He differs from Swift only in degree. He chuckles more, often using his talent for a play on words, though we hope that Swift often had his tongue pressed closely to his cheek when he spoke. Joyce clothed his genius in the garments of a literary Picasso. Harsh and unique in tone as in form, it appeals to the intellect and not to the heart and, while varying in degree only, it remains true in principle to the cold classical standards erected by the dean. It is only in our poetry and humorous plays that the more gentle literary arts have escaped the mantle of Swift—in the fun and mirth of Sheridan and Wilde and in the poignant nostalgic beauty of some of the poetry of Goldsmith, Mangan and Yeats.

CONCLUSION

In spite of the centuries that have passed and the many commentaries that have been published the enigma of Swift remains. He covered his personal movements with a cloak of great secrecy from the start. Nobody knows for certain where he was born or who was his father. No one can tell whether an impediment of kin forbade his union with Stella or whether, in fact, they were formally married in the deanery. His exact relationship with Vanessa remains unanswered. The character of his illness has been the subject of endless speculation although it seems clear that he was a tortured man whose melancholy and despondency grew steadily more acute and which ended in the darkness of a living death years before the grave.* The precise meaning of his clear lucid prose continues to receive fresh interpretation, while the stature of his genius alone remains unquestioned.

It is a matter of great significance that the important parts of this personal and emotional drama, as well as the writing of his greatest literary creation and his defence of human liberty took place within the heart, or the environs, of the ancient city of Dublin.

*Medical specialists today believe that Swift was suffering from Ménière's disease—a disturbance of the semicircular canals in the ear, which was the cause of Swift's symptoms of giddiness and vertigo. The actual cause of his death was probably senility.

NOTES

1. Maurice Craig, *Dublin 1660–1860*, pp. 4 and 5.
2. Ibid., p. 10.
3. Ibid., p. 11.
4. Ibid., p. 21.
5. Ibid., p. 50.
6. Denis Johnston, *In Search of Swift*.
7. R. Wyse Jackson, *Jonathan Swift, Dean and Pastor*, pp. 12 and 24.
8. Morris Bishop, *Petrarch and his World*, pp. 126 and 136.
9. Harold Williams (editor), *Journal to Stella*, Letter, March 19, 1711.
10. F. Elrington Ball (editor), *The Correspondence of Jonathan Swift*.
11. Herbert Davis, *Jonathan Swift, Essays on his Satire*, p. 26.
12. Ibid., p. 110.
13. Ibid., p. 23.

SELECT BIBLIOGRAPHY

Bernard Ackworth, *Swift*, London, 1947.
Sybil Le Brocquy, *Cadenus*, Dublin 1962.

The Beauty of Classical Dublin

It is mainly through the influence of the Greeks that European culture developed its own particular form of art. At an early date the aesthetic quality of Greek thought became evident in the *Iliad* when the poet, with fine descriptive power and a natural grace of language, created one of the epics of literature. Through the ages poems and dramas of this ancient myth-making people have provided inspiration for creative writers including Dante and Petrarch, Goethe and Shelley, while the ideas of Plato and Aristotle and the story and death of Socrates remain always new in spite of the centuries.

As with literature and thought, so too with the visual arts of architecture and sculpture. It is true that, long before the foundation of Athens and Rome, many of the pyramids, obelisks, temples and sphinxes of Egypt were beginning to assume the mellowness of age. The Greeks, in all likelihood, borrowed the idea of their early massive Doric columns and entablature from Egypt and Asia, but they developed and perfected a form of poetry in stone culminating in the Greek temple which has been described by Nikolaus Pavsner as the most perfect example ever achieved of architecture finding its expression in bodily beauty.[1] In it there was an artistic achievement of unity reflecting life in its most radiant light of shape and form. The ideal world of beauty was fulfilled in which there was nothing harrowing, nothing obscure, nothing blurred.

Rome made new departures and created new orders of architecture which were but variations of the originals but, to the Greeks, fell the role of inventing the grammar of conventional forms upon which so much of subsequent

European architecture was based. With the Renaissance and the neo-classical era of the 18th and 19th centuries, Greek and Roman architectural forms were revived and adopted in many cities of Europe and the Anglo-Saxon world. It was precisely during these latter centuries that Dublin developed into a capital in the full tide of this revival and from which she received her outline and character with fine Palladian buildings of stone scattered about among the brick streets and squares of the Georgian city.

THE NATURE OF GREEK AND ROMAN ARCHITECTURE

It is necessary, to consider at some considerable length, the essential features of classical art so that the lovely details of 18th century Dublin may be more readily understood.

In the architecture of Greece and Rome a column or pilaster, with its base, shaft and capital, and the entablature (the horizontal beam) above it consisting of architrave, frieze and cornice, was classified into one of the three recognised orders of architecture, viz., the Doric, Ionic and Corinthian with the later Tuscan and Composite orders which were merely variations of the earlier ones. The term *orders*, which appears so frequently in Greek, Roman and Renaissance architecture and which has relevance to so many buildings in classical Dublin, appears to have been first introduced into English about 1563 when the manual by Vitruvius came into general use in a translation from the Latin. In brief his system provides rules for architectural design based upon the proportions of three standard types of columns together with their bases, capitals and the entablatures which they support. They are named respectively after the three regions of Greece — Doris, Ionia and Corinthos in which they originated.

The Doric order is the oldest and sturdiest of the three.

Its fluted column has a capital consisting of a flat abacus resting on an echinus moulding. The entablature consists of three members — architrave, frieze and cornice. The frieze itself is ornamented by triglyphs (called from the Greek words meaning three slits) which are vetical projections decorated with a series of vertical grooves. These triglyphs are imitations in stone of the ends of those beams which, in the days of wooden construction, used to cross from side to side of the building. Two forms of cornice were used with varying rows of projecting blocks which had an ornamental purpose only and one of the rewarding sights in classical buildings is the variety and subtle distinction of the mouldings used for decoration and finish.

During the centuries of its development the basic elements of the Doric order did not change although columns became taller and more slender and the entasis or curved taper more and more delicate. This entasis in classical architecture is the almost imperceptible and amazingly subtle convex tapering of a column, with a slight swelling towards the middle, in order to correct the optical illusion of concavity created by simple tapering.

The Ionic order has a more slender column and a curious capital with spiral "volutes" or scrolls beneath its abacus. These are the ends of a band represented as passing horizontally across the top of the echinus and winding up on either side in a volute. The capital is thus rectangular and the volutes of the two faces of the capital are connected by a generally cylindrical form known as a cushion. The order achieved its refined perfection in the lovely temple of Nike Apteros and the Erechteum in Athens. The Ionic order is, in fact, one of the most graceful achievements of Greek art. The volute or scroll of this order was a favourite form of Palladio, Inigo Jones and others down to the present century. It is the most harmonious link between shaft and architrave that has been conceived and it is the combination of unity and variety in the spiral of its volutes, with the motion and play of curve generally, which constitutes the formal grace of the capital. It disdains the use of natural ornament whether of leaf or flower and

39

depends for its acceptance on beauty born of pure form.

The Corinthian column is the most slender of the three and has a capital which is much deeper than in those of the Doric or Ionic orders and which consists of a generally bell-shaped core the surface of which is surrounded by a characteristic decoration of acanthus leaves. It expresses a display of wealth and richness by the natural luxuriance of its capital. The Greeks however largely avoided imitating natural forms of beauty. Their execution aimed at smoothness and refinement and this was carried to such and extent that, to European ideas of architectural charm, there is something cold although fascinating in the elegant repose and finish of Greek civic art. It excites more admiration than affection — rather similar to the personal reaction towards classical Dublin where the dignity of the fine stone buildings and the streets and squares has the coldness of formality which lacks the warmth of cities like Vienna, Innsbruck or Seville. The Greeks had a feeling towards the aesthetic finish of their public buildings such as a poet might feel for the music of certain words. They sought perfection although their adornment was more in beauty of proportion than in picturesque ornamentation.[2]

The Romans borrowed all three orders from the Greeks with certin modifications and they especially favoured the Corinthian, the use of which on a monumental scale became the Roman order *par excellence*. The completely developed Corinthian form was magnificent and with the use of arches and domes these buildings acquired a grandeur which may still be seen in the Pantheon. Another element of Roman architecture was the placing of statues which were laid upon pedestals and base blocks high up on the building with the object probably of varying the outline of the structures and indicating the purposes for which they were erected. Statues were also placed on columns and the desire for sculpture led to the invention of the niche or recess with its semi-dome termination wholly unknown to the Greeks. In our own classical buildings of stone the use of sculpture on the pediments and the presence of the niche have been faithfully copied and the erection of columns for the former statue of Nelson and for the phoenix monument have had their Roman precedent. Both the design and use of the ancient orders were altered by the Romans and their form of Doric differs from the Greek in many elements with its dissimilar capital, the absence of fluting in the columns and the presence of a moulded base.[3] The printing house in Trinity College is a charming example of the Roman Doric while the facades of Kings Inn's library, St. Andrew's Westland Row and the Pro-Cathedral are copies of the Greek.

THE RENAISSANCE AND THE CLASSICAL REVIVAL

During the Dark Ages and the period of medieval Gothic splendour the classical forms of Greece and Rome fell into abeyance. The Italians of the 14th century, however, sought to revive their splendid past and to create a new era of art. In no place was this feeling of confidence so intense as in Florence. There Brunelleschi pioneered the revival of Roman art not by copying the ancient monuments but by the adoption of a new way of building in which the forms of classical art were freely used to create modes of harmony and form. If Brunelleschi sought the development of a new architectural era, he certainly succeeded and, with him, the great rebirth of classical forms of beauty was commenced.

The style which followed the Renaissance and which flourished in the Catholic areas of Europe is usually called the Baroque. Apart from the ornate display of detail, it is not always easy to identify it externally and, from the Renaissance almost up to the present day, architects have used the same basic forms of columns, pilasters, cornices, entablatures and mouldings, all of which were originally borrowed from ancient ruins. In 18th century Dublin we have the clear outline of a city of the classical revival with Renaissance overtones and with many fine details of Baroque and Rococo art in the internal decoration of the mansions and homes.

41

In the 16th century that remarkable manual by Vitruvius, *De Re Architectura*, having been printed and translated into several languages, became, in many respects, the architects's bible. Vitruvius had been a Roman architect during the reign of Augustus and his text is still valuable for its accurate information. Palladio, a native of Vicenza, also had a strong influence on the course of architecture in Europe and in these islands for two centuries after his death in 1580. He made an intensive study of classical literature and of the ancient buildings of Rome and it was his great literary work *I quattro libri dell' Architetura* which was the main cause of his influence. His palatial buildings in Vicenza were of great significance and transformed that quiet Italian town into one of the most interesting period cities of Europe. If the ancient world was the source from which classical Dublin took its 18th century form, Palladio and his disciples were primarily the driving force behind this creation. A visit to his native city, now in the mature charm of its lovely classical detail, recalls the many buildings in Dublin and throughout the country of which Vicenza was the creative source. In England, Inigo Jones also studied the remains of ancient Rome with the aid of Palladio's treatise. He took as his criterion of excellence the Roman version of the orders and brought to England a critical appreciation of antiquity. It is thus mainly the Roman and Renaissance interpretation of classical art which Dublin inherited during the era of its revival. Here, Palladianism, as it was called, flourished brilliantly for some thirty years and produced two or three at least of its finest monuments. Such was the carrying power of this great movement which started in the little city of Vicenza that it penetrated to Germany, Poland, Russia and to the remotest corner of the English-speaking world.[4]

CLASSICAL DUBLIN

Among the many anomalies in Dublin we find that one of

42

its earliest classical monuments was built without either columns or pilasters. The fine library of Trinity College, which was the creation of Thomas Burgh, and was opened in 1732, is the oldest example in the city of a building which has the Greek purity of outline without the usual detail of the classical portico or facade. It possesses a stark organic beauty in the basic meaning of that term, being itself ornamental and without the need for ornamentation. The fundamental principles of position and construction have been adhered to and the quality of its stone illustrates the truth that fabric as much as form is an ingredient from which the aesthetic is born. Stone and brick are living things which mellow with age unlike modern plastic materials which need ornamentation or paint to hide their basic ugliness. In personality the library possesses an unusual blending of the classical Greek and the ultra-modern without the columns of the ancient or the steel and concrete of the present- day world. It is almost a plain building with projections only at the centre and the ends to break the clarity of its rectangular form while the balustrade and the exquisite mouldings of the cornice, almost invisible in relation to the great bulk of the walls, betray its only concession to ornamental forms. Together with the charming early 18th century Marsh's library with its high pitched roof and old-world atmosphere across the close from Swift's cathedral and the solid granite building at King's Inns with Greek Doric facade and reading room of the Ionic order, Burgh's great edifice possesses a wealth of rare books which places Dublin high in the company of Europe's intellectual centres.

The architect's last important building was Dr. Steven's hospital with its arcaded courtyard which quaintly recalls Robinson's fine Royal Hospital at Kilmainham. The main doorway, with its arch and semi-circular pediment, and the clock-tower and wrought-iron give a human aspect to the building which is rare in the more perfected classical forms and which, with its stucco exterior, immediately place the hospital within the more humane Italian tradition of domestic art and not within the strict traditions of the 18th century rule of taste. Not far away is the dignified pedimented front of St. Patrick's Hospital, built from the donation of Jonathan Swift, while St. Catherine's Church in Thomas Street presents its crumbling granite facade of Roman Doric with particularly fine pediment, Ionic portico and the noble proportions of the columns.

The real high street of Dublin consists of that long line of streets running from Christ Church Cathedral in the heart of the former walled city eastwards to Trinity College and its green. The street runs gracefully around the curved colonnade of the former parliament house on its way over O'Connell Bridge to the north, and curves more sharply to the right through Grafton and Nassau streets on its way south. It is here in the very centre of the city where the roads from the hinterland meet in College Green that two of the most important classical buildings and three of Dublin's most attractive statues adorn the heart of the city.

The most interesting Palladian building in Ireland is the old Parliament House. It originally comprised a House of Lords and a House of Commons of which the Lords has survived with little alteration behind Gandon's fine Corinthian portico. The monumental grandeur of the south colonnade with the exquisite curviture of the main building and the recessed courtyard and portico embellished with pediments and niches, statues and balustrade, plaques and medallions and with the silken-gray of the Portland stone becoming silver in the sunlight — all give to the edifice an impression of movement and the character of a Roman monument which has been embellished by the finishing school of the Renaissance.

The forest of columns, both attached and free, which encircle the entire face of the building and which is lacking in Burgh's college library provides the main aesthetic appeal of this splendid monument. The fact that the Ionic volutes are not in the pure Greek rectangular form but project from the corner of the capitals and that the columns of the east portico are of the Composite order, with surmounted statues, does not in the least destroy the classical character of the architecture. Coming from the Renaissance ideas of Palladio and his pupils, with Edward Lovett Pearce as the main architect, one could not expect that the formal purity of Greek taste would have been preserved. The semi-circular outline of the building, together with its rich colonnade, its porticoes and niches, declare it to be essentially an epic of Roman classical art which has been modified to suit the needs of a later century of taste.[5]

The west front of Trinity College occupies the most commanding architectural site in Dublin standing at a point where the main flow of north-south traffic sweeps past and facing the city's busiest commercial street. It is perhaps the most dignified piece of collegiate architecture in these islands with its fine arrangement of windows, its columns and pilasters of the composite order so dear to the architects of the revival, and its excellent corner pavilions, with the entire facade showing a harmonious blend of Portland stone and granite often glowing in the evening sunlight. In front, the statues of Burke and Grattan add dignity to the Green but it is the statue of Goldsmith that recalls, affectionately, the fact that here in Dublin there once lived for a while a poet with one of the most beautiful minds that ever passed through the strange by-ways of literature.

As a functional unit the Castle is the best classical essay in brick which Dublin possesses and which dates, in its present form, from the mid-18th century. As the seat of power it gradually changed its appearance from the stone of the medieval fortress to the more intimate brick facade of the later century. With its few surviving towers and the commanding nature of the site, it still possesses an aspect of authority which is emphasised by the presence of the gates of Justice and Mars with their statues crowning the segmental pediments of the arches. The spacious aspect of the area reflects the later dignity of Georgian streets and squares and the character of the state apartments and St. Patrick's Hall has many a parallel among the city mansions and professional centres of the capital. But it is the internal finish of the lovely Gothic Chapel Royal with its wood carving, its atmosphere and the ever-so-gentle beauty of its vaulted ceiling which vies for prominence with the exquisite Palladian facade of the former Office of Arms, its tower and cupola flanked by the mythological gateways of War and Peace.

Adjoining are the elegant classical buildings of the former Newcomen's bank and the City Hall which notionally appear to act as outer defences for the protection of the castle. The former adds to a worthy site a facade of sensitive feminine charm. Built of Portland stone, which has mellowed gracefully with the years, it has a softness of triglyph, chain and moulding expressed with an almost Greek finesse, while the balustrade, recesses and medallions express the later culture of Rome. In the artistic sense, the building is a poem in stone and a lyric poem too. Thomas Ivory's other great creation is the former Blue-Coat School in Blackhall Place which, with its centre-piece of the Ionic order, its sea-green cupola, the elegant pavilions and the gentle curvature of the wings, was one of the least known of Dublin's attractive buildings because of the quiet corner in which it stands.

Thomas Cooley's Royal Exchange, now the City Hall, was built on a square of one hundred feet and has two handsome porticoes of the Corinthian order, the one facing Parliament Street being pedimented but without sculpture and having double columns at the extremities while the other, facing Castle Street, is surmounted by the architrave, freize and cornice of its order over which is a balustrade carried round the building. The internal plan is that of a circle inscribed within a square with twelve composite fluted columns penetrated by subsidiary Ionic columns supporting an entablature with a dome resting upon its drum, and with an ambulatory stretching out into the rest of the square. It is lighted by a central opening in the dome after the style of the Pantheon at Rome with additional circular windows through which the sunlight pours into the mellow interior with its elaborately-worked stucco, its murals, and the fine statues of Dr. Lucas and Thomas Drummond, of O'Connell and Thomas Davis. The present rotunda-shaped plan makes a fine central hall and may be one of the most beautiful halls of its kind in Europe.[6]

James Gandon's great compositions of the Four Courts and the Customs House may be studied together, linked as they are by one architectural mind in its varying moods and by the long line of the Liffey spanned by graceful stone bridges and protected by sturdy granite walls. In outline the former is monumental and masculine with the prosaic grandeur of Rome while the latter is a poetic feminine creation of the Renaissance lying horizontal to the river front and in harmony with the ships that used to berth along its quay. The granite fabric of the Four Courts — its Corinthian order with pediment and statues, the central mass with colonnaded drum and low curved roof externally, without the final grace of a lantern dome, classify it as a monument of almost barbaric classical power. In the great circular hall, however, with its arrangement of courts, in the splendid portico with its deeply-curved porch and in the recessed areas between the wings, the real charm of the building lies with the added adornment of medallion and plaque.[7]

Facing the old city on the hill with the domed outline of Adam and Eve's and the fortress-like bulk of St. Audoen's hiding its stately Corinthian portico near Christ Church and the ancient tower and arch of the medieval city, the slender line of the quay is broken by this fine building with startling emphasis half-way on its journey from Kingsbridge to the sea.

With the graceful line broken only by a fine Doric portico and by side pavilions of exquisite proportions adorned by Grecian urns and coats of arms, by medallion and moulding, the Customs House radiates a Palladian distinction. Built around two courtyards, it has a finely composed river front with a dome closely modelled upon that of Greenwich. The whole conception, whether viewed from Beresford Place or from across the river, has a Greek purity of form with the additional Italian charm of personality and poise.

Gandon's third major work in Dublin is King's Inns. The curved triumphal-arch approach from Henrietta Street still retains the Lion and Unicorn while the great bulk of the Dining Hall and Registry of Deeds borders this approach from the east. The west front presents a refined pattern of the Ionic order with medallions and plaques forming a welcome addition to pediments, colonnade and cupola.[8] The beautiful little dome sits with poise upon its base and presents an example of one of Dublin's most charming features when the tiny domes of the city are glinting in the sun at Mount Street Crescent and Francis Street, at the Rotunda, Mercer's Hospital and Arran Quay.

GEORGIAN DUBLIN

Towards the middle of the 18th century the external appearance of Dublin's more elegant streets began to resemble those of London and, if the essential requirement in domestic art is to capture the spirit of rest, and to express it in house-design and appointments, Georgian Dublin achieved this on the grand scale. The clear-cut form of both street and square preserves the Greek purity of line while, occasionally, a palatial building is incorporated into the general plan and shows its superior dignity with a stone facade or double frontage in brick.

The Georgian city house, which is the domestic expression of the classical revival, usually has a uniformity of shape and style, if not of size. Built of red or yellow brick its charm lies in numbers when formed into a medium-sized street or square. Granite steps lead up to a panelled doorway with a fan-light often beautifully ribbed and glazed and with wooden or stone columns of the Doric or Ionic order ornamenting the sides. Sometimes elongated side windows add harmony to a clear vertical line, while the technique of window-arrangement in the facade avoids monotony with variety of shape which reaches maturity in the tall and graceful line of the drawing-room storey. In autumn, or through the mantle of a thickening fog or mist, when night has fallen on the older streets and suburban roads, Dublin acquires once again the atmosphere of a colonial town when, with the transformation of light and shade, a new, and often lovely, detail is born under a darkening sky or beneath the Baroque canopy of the stars.

It is the variation in detail, however, which gives fascination to the study of Georgian Dublin. Often the doorway is surmounted by a triangular or semi-circular pediment, sometimes with cornice and moulding, which varies in size and form like the proportions of the fan-light. Sometimes pilasters are used in place of columns while the wrought-iron balconies, which have survived in many houses, create the atmosphere of a southern city. Sometimes, too, the railings for the area or the steps acquire a more pronounced character or curve in harmony with the contour of the pavement or the nature of the building. At times the steps project on to the path with a haughty disdain for the pedestrian while here and there the older lamp standards, with their attractive form and colour, have been preserved and the surviving granite pavements always give solidity and colour to the pathways with their changing patterns of shade in the sunlight and in the rain. Above all it is the varying mood of the seasons which gives charm to the clear classical outline of the city. In a spring or autumn morning, when the heavens are young, Georgian Dublin becomes a worthy and a welcoming capital and the outline and colour of both street and square express the tone of a rose-red town in a mould that is truly European. When the snows of winter have crowned Kippure and Kilmashogue and the air is clear with the sharp tang of frost then the silhouette of the city, crowned by the homely bulk of its chimneys and by the spires and domes, as seen against the cold blue of a short evening twilight, becomes a lovely work of art which is born from the happy blending of light and shade and the clear-cut lines of the classical era of taste. For a time one can only stand and gaze as the ideal world of beauty is born again as in the days of Pericles and in which there is "nothing harrowing, nothing obscure, nothing blurred."[9]

The grand extent of Merrion Square is saved from uniformity by its fine park and by the open space of Leinster Lawn while the limestone and granite fabric of parliament, museum and gallery provides a variation on the theme of brick. A characteristic view of what is best in Georgian Dublin may be seen at the junction of this street and square. To the east Upper Mount Street culminates in the crescent and St. Stephen's Church showing the gem-like beauty of its perfect Ionic portico and the tower and cupola which make it one of the best loved of Dublin's churches. To the west the ensemble of fine buildings of the arts and of science, together with Trinity College, provide a real cultural centre for the city, while the cosy cul-de-sac of Ely Place shows Georgian Dublin in a mood of snugness and homely charm. A rather similar note is struck in the case of Parnell Square where the line of doorways and red brick is broken to advantage by the curvature and limestone facade of Charlemount House and the sparkling granite of the church while the Rotunda and the Gate Theatre incorporate elements of the clearest classical style. Fitzwilliam Square is, however, the most intimate in the purity of its form, its detail and its tone while the green of the park forms a vivid contrast with the mellow brick when caressed by the changing colours of an autumn day.

In spite of change St. Stephen's Green still preserves some of the finest mansions and is adorned by the blending of brick and stone with dwellinghouses, churches and mansions sometimes standing side by side and forming the facade of a noble square. University Church, like the Chapel Royal, is one of the really charming shrines of the city and, while the former preserves a classical tradition, both possess a loveliness of form and detail, an atmosphere and a story which is appreciated by all who understand the language of history and of art. The elegant stone fronts of Newman and Iveagh house are worthy of their interiors with stairways, ceilings and walls carved or decorated in the Baroque ideal and enriched with stucco and Rococo plasterwork which here, as elsewhere in the city, has exceeded anything of its period in England.

Much of the internal stuccowork in Dublin was done by immigrants, notably Paul and Philip Francini and Bartholomew Cramillion. In fact, Cramillion's exotic interior of the Rotunda Hospital chapel is unique in Ireland in its flamboyant Rubens-like symbolism which gives us a link with the rich Rococo art of central and southern Europe. This art is the product of the Catholic world. It is an acquired aesthetic taste at variance with the organic purity of the ancients or the puritanical formalism of the Anglo-Saxon classical revival. The whole movement started from the basic forms of the Greek and Roman world. The Renaissance injected into it a new life and gave it a freedom of expression with overtones of its own. The neo-classical era of the English-speaking world remained true to the idealism of Palladio and the ancients, particularly with interiors, when a church was designed mainly as a hall where the faithful met for common worship while, in the sunny Catholic world of Europe's heartland, the dazzling internal pageantry of the churches, with the pomp and display of precious stones, of gold and stucco, were used deliberately to express a vision of heavenly glory.

The wheel of fortune in the artistic world had turned full circle from the organic beauty of a Greek temple to the full-blooded detail of a Baroque interior and, in our strange amalgam of a city, there are many examples of a facade or internal finish which express, in varying degrees, the ideals of these apparently conflicting realms of art. The Ionic and Doric churches, respectively, of Gardiner Street and Westland Row contained rich Baroque altars with Baroque or stucco ceilings, while others adorn the classical churches of St. Audoen's and Arran Quay. The more refined Rococo decoration of Belvedere House and the College of Surgeons, of No. 20 Dominick Street and Newman House, are among the hidden glories of the city while the fine halls and internal doorways, cornices and plaques, stairways and stately reception rooms to be seen everywhere in classical Dublin, form a large part of our heritage and contribute to its total wealth proportionately to the rich treasures of our libraries, to the stately facade of street and square with tower, spire and dome presenting a traditional landmark against the rigid skyline, to the protective curve of the bay, and the long serrated line of hills which gives attraction to the city when approaching it from the sea.

NOTES

1. Nikolaus Pavsner, *An Outline of European Architecture*, p. 19.
2. Sir Banister Fletcher, *A History of Architecture*, pp. 68-108; Martin S. Briggs, *Everyman's Concise Encyclopaedia of Architecture*, p. 20; *The Irish Builder*, 1859, 1864, 1879-89 and 1894; *Encyclopaedia Britannica*, 11th ed., vol. 10, p. 798 and vol. 16, p. 854.
3. Sir Banister Fletcher, *op. cit.*, pp. 141-155; Martin S. Biggs, *op. cit.*, p. 21; *The Irish Builder*, 1881, 1886, 1887 and 1889; Encyclopaedia Britannica, 11th ed., vol 16, p. 854 and vol. 19, p. 391. All that needs to be known about the history and the nature of Greek and Roman Architecture will be found in the volumes referred to at reference notes 1 and 2 above.
4. Martin S. Briggs, *op. cit.*, pp. 25, 238 and 358.
5. John Summerson, *Architecture in Britain, 1530-1830*, pp. 197 and 227-229.
6. John Summerson, *op. cit.*, pp. 272-274; *The Irish Builder*, 1859 and 1867.
7. Maurice Craig, *Dublin 1660-1860*, p. 250.
8. John Summerson, *op. cit.*, pp. 272-274.
9. Nikolaus Pavsner, *op. cit.*, p. 19.

SELECT BIBLIOGRAPHY

Sir Banister Fletcher, *A History of Architecture*, London, 1924.
John Summerson, *Architecture in Britain, 1530-1830*, London, 1953.
Maurice Craig, *Dublin 1660-1860*, Dublin, 1952.
Nikolaus Pavsner, *An Outline of European Architecture*, Middlesex, 1943.
The Dublin Builder and *The Irish Builder*, Dublin, 1859-1895.
Martin S. Briggs, *Everyman's Concise Encyclopaedia of Architecture*, London, 1959.
Encyclopaedia Britannica, 11th ed., vols. 10, 16 and 19.

Along the Liffey Shore

The source of the river is near Liffey Head bridge in a remote area of bog in the townland of Powerscourt Mountain in County Wicklow. This spot is as desolate as the most ascetic hermit could wish and is about half way between upper Lough Bray and Sally Gap. In the vicinity are the sources also of the Dargle and the Annamoe rivers while to the north rise the Dodder and the Glencree. With Kippure to the west and Tonduff and Maulin to the east, this area of bleak moorland would appear to be a natural basin for the collection and distribution of these mountain waters.

The journey upwards from Rathfarnham continues through Willbrook and Ballyboden to an area rich in stone circles and dolmens within view of Mount Venus, with its megalithic tomb, Mount Pelier, with the ruins of the Hell-Fire club, and Cruagh, Killakee and Glendoo mountains until one reaches the old reformatory and the war cemetery at Glencree. Here one must pause, because the view towards Knockree is one of great charm where the mixed woodlands of the valley, with gorse and hawthorn, blend with the pine trees of the hills and further east are the Sugar Loaf mountain and the sea.

The most dramatic feature along this road is provided by the two Loughs Bray each of which would appear to have been excavated from the base of Kippure and almost enclosed within an amphitheatre of rock. With the dark brown of the water and the soaring height of the Eagle's Craig the beautiful cottage *ornée*, which stands beside the enchanting lower lake and which is protected by tall trees, presents a romantic picture against the sombre background of the cliffs.

THE RIVER IN WICKLOW

About two miles beyond Lough Bray the Liffey emerges from its cradle of turf as a little brown stream. It gathers speed quickly within its banks of peat and mountain soil while heather and rushes, mosses and rough grass grow along the edges. Sometimes the water glides swiftly over its bed and then again it murmurs and gurgles or sings loud or softly in answer to the changing nature of the terrain. One September afternoon of sunshine and showers I stood at the bridge listening to the music of the water and watching the changing colours of the day. Occasionally great white clouds appeared on the horizon and, assuming fascinating forms, they kissed the mountains one by one as they wandered across the sky.

The stream grows in volume quickly as several brooks discharge into it. When the second bridge is reached it is already a small river flowing rapidly over the granite rocks of its bed and banks. Now the gorse appears and large areas of fern cover the adjacent fields as the river is joined by the Carrigvore and Lugnalee brooks near the coronation plantation and the woods of Kippure estate. It travels along by splendid beech, oak and pine trees and the sylvan character of the scenery now commences and continues for most of the course on its journey to the sea.

The first object of antiquarian interest is the moat at Athdown which stands near a rivulet that descends from Seefingan mountain. On the lower slope of Seefingan is a large cairn and, on the summit of Seefin, is a round cairn covering a cruciform passage grave. Soon the river is joined by the Ballylow and Ballydonnell brooks whose waters descend from Gravale mountain and from Mullagh-cleevaun, that lonely queen of the wilderness. The stream then hastens over a channel of granite rocks at the foot of delicate birch trees and under Ballysmuttan bridge towards the beautiful cascade at Cloghleagh. Here we must pause again to watch the lovely Shankill river tumbling down from its hill through a tunnel and over a rocky glen darkened by mature trees until it glides over its bed of shalestone under the great arch of the bridge and into the Liffey. With the quiet country church nearby and a background of broad fields and woods the mad rush of the Shankill through its dark glen and the stark beauty of the bridge distinguish Cloghleagh as one of the alluring places along the river.

The flow now become more gentle as it passes under the shade of thick plantations which descend to the water's edge akin to the woodland rivers of Germany or Austria. It proceeds along placidly towards Manor Kilbride but suddenly changes it course and goes in a south westerly direction before meeting the waters of the Brittas river near Ballyward bridge after that tributary had flowed under the bridge and through the woods of Kilbride House. In this parish are two burial grounds and several raths and in the townland of Threecastles stand the remains of a 15th century castle which has been partly restored. It is traditionally accepted as having been one of three, the other two having long since disappeared.

The river now approaches the great modern reservoir which extends southwards beyond Ballyknockan up to the bridge at Pollaphuca. In former times a marked variation in the flow existed between the wet months and the dry and this variation could be serious during times of flood. North of the bridge the river ran in a deep valley and emerged through a gorge. It was thus decided to control the upper area because there the ground seemed to have been naturally intended for a large artificial lake and a dam across the gorge would result in many million cubic feet of water being held in storage. An increased head would be obtained and the entire river could be controlled with a regular flow during summer and winter in wet years and in dry. It is now accepted that a large lake existed in pre-historic times in the valley and the building of the reservoir amounted in effect to a partial restoration of the lake.

The Liffey is a steep river especially in the upper part of its course. It rises at an elevation of about 1715 feet. In the first eight miles it falls by 1075 feet whereas in the last fifty miles it falls by only 375 feet to tidal waters at Islandbridge weir near Kilmainham. An old name for the river was Ruirtheach — the rushing waters. The distance from its source to the city centre is only thirteen miles as the crow flies, whereas its actual circuitous course through three counties is seventy four miles to tidal waters.[1] Its most important tributary is the King's river which rises in the Wicklow Gap at the foot of Tonelagee and not far from lovely Lough Ouler. It also has a steep fall from its source but, with the formation of the reservoir, about half of that river has become submerged.

The first town which we reach is Blessington. The manor was created by Charles II for one of the Boyle family who erected the church about 1682. In 1778 the manor devolved on Lord Hillsborough, who later became the Marquis of Downshire. Today it has an attractive granite fountain and market house and in the churchyard at Burgage may be seen St. Mark's Cross. This cross was removed from a nearby monastic site which is now submerged. Opposite the hotel are the wooded hills of the former demesne while, along the shore of the lake, beautiful beech and pine trees flourish and several places have been established for scenic views with seats and swards of grass. On the east side in the townland of Lackan is a small ruined chambered cairn and an early monastic site with St.Boodin's grave and a well which was once famed for its cures.

A peninsula divides the lake south of Blessington and, at its northern tip, stands Baltyboys House embosomed in beech trees with views over undulating wooded hills and sloping fields. Further south is the splendid mansion of Tulfarris by whose parkland the river in former days rapidly gained in volume as it collected its forces for the great plunge at Pollaphuca. The main road from Blessington continues alongside Russborough with its peerless treasures of architecture and art. In a setting of rich woodlands the mansion was built of silver-gray granite which glitters in the sunlight and it is perhaps the most perfect example in Ireland of Palladian style. Over the hill is Barrettstown Castle where members of the government occasionally meet for consultation. Now the road adjoins the lake and five miles further on is Alexander Nimmo's beautiful ornamental bridge at Pollaphuca which consists of one pointed arch with a span of 65 feet springing from the rocks at either side. The river plunges 150 feet in three stages but the new dam has greatly reduced the volume of the falls as most of the water is directed underground to the Liffey powerhouse. As early as the 18th century the waterfall was a scenic attraction and, in Lewis's *Topographical Dictionary of Ireland*, the former condition of the cascade was described as consisting of three successive waterfalls 150 feet in height. When the river was swollen by heavy rains the water rushed down with tumultuous impetuosity into a circular basin of the rock worn quite smooth and of great depth the form of which imparted to it the motion of a whirlpool and from which the cascade derived its name. It then dashed through narrow openings in the rocks and formed two more falls the lowest being about 50 feet high.

It is probable that belief in the existence of fairies came into Ireland with the earliest colonies. The púca represents an odd mixture of merriment and malignity and, under the name of Puck, he will be remembered as the merry wanderer of night. Several places are associated with the name and they are generally wild lonely dells, caves or chasms in rocks on the sea-shore or pools in deep glens which are suitable haunts for this mysterious sprite. He is often found lurking in raths and lisses. Several old forts throughout the country are called Rathpooka or Lissaphuca and, in a dreary spot at the foot of the Ballyhoura mountains, Castlepook was considered a suitable home for that strange spirit of night.

Today the Liffey flows sluggishly in the deep glen the sides of which are steep and covered with ferns and thick woodland. Nearby is a row of mature beech trees whose smooth silver bark reflects the sunlight and whose roots embrace the entire fence and spread across the path while mountain breezes play hide-and-seek among the leaves creating music with those sylvan castanets.

THE RIVER IN KILDARE

The river now turns sharply northwest and enters County Kildare. To the south is the moat of Knockshee and in the townland of Broadleas Commons is a Bronze Age stone circle known as *The Piper's Stones* of which 27 completed stones and 12 fragments survive. A few miles west of the reservoir is the Liffey-side village of Ballymore Eustace which takes its name from the Anglo-Norman family of FitzEustace who were amongst the great landowners of the county for several centuries. In the Protestant church is an ancient font and an early 16th century armoured tomb effigy of one of the family. In the churchyard may be seen a granite high cross, a smaller granite cross and the remains of the ancient church. Formerly a castle of great strength existed here but its fabric has entirely disappeared. The Liffey now passes under an elegant stone bridge of six arches and on the north bank some miles to the west, in the parish of Coghlanstown, are the remains of the medieval church of St. James and its graveyard with fragments of of crosses and a holy well. It is traditionally believed that a monastery was founded here by monks from Santiago de Compostela in Spain and that they gave their name also to the nearby parish of Jago. Two other holy wells associated with St. James exist in the county.

The journey is now through beautiful wooded countryside into the land of stud farms and stately homes which continue through the valley in this traditional racing domain of the Curragh and Kildare. We pass Ardinode House and Stonebrook and then by Gilltown and Ragusa all of which are sheltered and embellished by splendid lime and beech trees in a setting of well-kept fields and lawns. Later, through the estate of lovely Harristown House and under Brannockstown bridge, the river proceeds onwards towards Kilcullen. On a warm October morning I stood on the old bridge at Harristown watching the brown stream pass under its canopy of broad-leaved deciduous trees with little sand banks here and there and wild flowers clutching at the edges. Apart from the sound of flowing water there was only a silence of woods and of pasture while, occasionally, beech leaves fell and became copper coloured in the shadows. Horses sought for shade under two ancient lime trees and in the distance was the soft blue-gray of the hills. I thought of the Mughal emperor who had inscribed over his Hall of the Private Audience in Delhi the delectable couplet:

If on earth there is a garden of bliss
It is this, it is this, it is this.

That morning I would not have exchanged Harristown for the famed water-garden of the Mughal palace because the sylvan wanderings of the Liffey in its own season and setting have created one of the loveliest rivers in Ireland and perhaps in all the world:

Now silent now singing the never-ending flow
Tells its tale of mystery from ages long ago.

Some miles from the present town are the remains of Old Kilcullen on a magnificent hill site from which one has a clear view of the Wicklow mountains. It derives its name from the foundation there of a church and monastery in the 5th century. Although plundered by the Scandinavians the settlement was fortified with walls and gates by the Normans. A castle was erected by the Fitzmartin family and, in the early 14th century, a bridge was built over the river at the site of the present town. Under the name of Kilcullenbridge the town rapidly increased in importance and caused the decline of Old Kilcullen. These names are today commemorated by the separate townlands of Old Kilcullen and Kilcullenbridge. On Old Kilcullen hill may be seen the lofty base of a round tower and nearby is part of the shaft of a 9th or 10th century high cross with interlaced patterns and biblical subjects. Alongside this is an undecorated shaft of another cross the face of which is divided into panels.

Northwest of this medieval site on the summit of Knockaulin is the hill-fort of Dun Ailinne the central mound of which rises 200 feet above the plain and which is ringed by a massive earthen bank 15 feet high with a wide internal ditch. It dominated the centre of the fertile axis of ancient Leinster and is regarded as having been a ritual site used for periodic assemblies and a seat of political power in pre-Christian times along with Dinn Righ hill-fort in Carlow and Mullaghmast further south in Kildare. In his learned treatise, *Celtic Leinster*, Dr. Alfred P. Smyth states that this fort of Dun Ailinne, overlooking the Curragh, although deserted by the historical period, continued to symbolise the ancient glories of the Leinster-men taking its place in the national scene beside Tara, Aileach and Emain Macha. As late as the 16th and 17th centuries the court-poets of the O'Tooles and the O'Byrnes constantly referred in their eulogies to the ancient glories of the rich central plain which their chiefs had lost to the Normans four centuries earlier when they had been driven into the impenetrable wilderness of the mountains.[2] If you stand on the hill and look across the valley on a day in early summer when the hedges are heavy with blossoms and cattle are browsing in rich pastures or wandering from field to field over the trodden earth it is easy to understand the resentment of the Gaelic chiefs at the loss of their patrimony and to see why the Anglo- Normans considered that this was a land worth fighting for and a land in which they could plant their estates and establish their power.

One mile east of modern Kilcullen is New Abbey grave-yard beside the river. It marks the site of a Franciscan friary which was founded in the 15th century by Sir Roland FitzEustace of Harristown, the first Lord Portlester, who was for many years Lord Chancellor of Ireland. He was buried in the friary and an elaborate altar tomb of himself and his wife Margaret with effigies and panels was erected. It still survives although much defaced by weathering. Portlester had built a chapel in St. Audoen's in Dublin and he and his wife are also commemorated in the porch of that church by the double effigy of a tomb-cenotaph. At Kilcullen the river turns towards the north-west and within one mile it meanders past the elegant residence of Castlemartin. The present house dates from about 1730 and occupies the site and part of the castle which was one of the chief seats of the FitzEustace family from the 14th century. It is surrounded by a richly-wooded park with lawns and gardens and possesses 18th century wrought-iron arches, railings and entrance gates which rank amongst the finest in Ireland. There too is the sensitively-restored manorial church and altar tomb of the 15th century. The Liffey now proceeds through attractive scenery of plain and valley near willow, birch and alder groves with clusters of fern and wild flowers towards the five-arched stone bridge below Athgarvan House under which it flows placidly towards the modern town of Newbridge under which it flows placidly towards the modern town of Newbridge on the eastern side of the Curragh.

In his *Irish Names of Places* P.W. Joyce states that the word currach can mean a racecourse or a morass and that, in the former sense, it gives its name to the Curragh of Kildare which had been used as a racecourse from the most remote ages. History and tradition also tend to show that from an early period the Curragh was a common. It was an important assembly place in pre-Christian days. The sites of over 30 earth works have been found and these have been scientifically explored and mapped. Today, apart from mountain land, this great plain of 5,000 acres is the largest unenclosed area in the country and it preserves an appearance rather similar to that of early times.[3] The legendary Finn MacCumhaill and his warriors used it as their training ground near their camp on the Hill of Allen. In Christian times it became closely associated with St. Brigid and her community and, in the 12th century, it was described as "St. Brigid's pasture in which no plough was suffered to turn a furrow". In the *Descriptive*

Account of the County of Kildare, which was prepared for Sir William Petty by Thomas Monk about the year 1662, the following descripton of the area is given: "Near the centre of this county is the Curragh of Kildare, a large and spatious plaine and common to all the adjacent neighbourhood who find it a rich and commodius, as well as healthful, pasturage especially for sheep that bear a fine staple and the sweetest flesh of any in the kingdom it being thronged with flocks all year round. . . . Hither are also seen to come all the nobility and gentry of the kingdome that either pretends to love or delight in hawking and hunting or racing for in this clearer and finer aire the falcon goes to a higher pitch or mounts so as often to be scarce visible; the hounds enjoy the scent more freely and the courser in his swift carreare is less sensible of pressure or opposition than elsewhere".

Some distance to the north rises the Hill of Allen which possesses a circular tower with an internal staircase that was erected by Sir Gerald Aylmer in 1859. This hill is considered to have been the principal fortress of Finn MacCumhaill the legendary leader of the *fiana* or hunting bands whose exploits took place in the remote wilderness. The cycle of literature associated with him abounds in references to the wilderness and the woods and this Hill or Isle of Allen was in ancient times surrounded by bog and wood stretching for miles across the Irish Midlands.

At Newbridge the Liffey reaches its most westerly point after which it curves in a north-easterly direction through the wooded grounds of the college, past the demesne of Old Connell stud and then over the rich limestone land to the edge of Barrettstown House with its Gothic architecture and terraced lawns that sweep downwards towards the water. After one mile the river passes Morristown Lattin demesne with its mansion which was substantially rebuilt in Tudor style in 1845. The Liffey now approaches Victoria bridge, one of the many fine stone structures which lend fascination to the river along most of its journey from the source to the sea. Nearby is an old water-mill with part of the wheel *in situ* together with its mill-race which emerges from under its own special bridge. The mill house has been restored and the river banks are shaded by ash, sycamore and beech trees with occasional poplars and the wild willows that grow aslant the brook.

The next feature is Carragh bridge, a narrow although beautiful stone structure of six arches which was erected in 1861. Soon the river is crossed by the railway line near Sallins and, not far from the fine 18th century Osberstown House, nearby, is the splendid Leinster aqueduct which was built in 1780 and which carries the canal and a road over the Liffey. In the vicinity is lovely Sandymount House and, in a short time, the rich woods of Milicent come into view and we pass across the graceful and recently-restored bridge with its pedestrian recesses. This mansion was the early home of Sir Richard Griffith and, from its terraced lawn, one can hear the pleasant sound of the river flowing over its weir and under the shadow of mature deciduous trees that flourish along the banks. On the other side of the hill is the historic graveyard of Bodenstown. The Liffey proceeds in the quiet meandering way of lowland streams, brown and gray in turn with now and again the song of its rapids or the music of the weirs and water-courses of the plains.

It flows under the Romanesque arches of Alexandra bridge near the village of Clane where a monastery had been established at a very early period and adjacent to which are the remains of a 13th century Franciscan friary which was founded by one of the Fitzgerald family whose mutilated effigy may still be seen. In the village the Protestant church has been restored and to the south overlooking the river is a de Hereford motte to which the name Queen Buana's grave has been given in modern times. In his poem *Mesgedra* Sir Samuel Ferguson tells the legendary tale of the nobility, love and death of the queen. Mesgedra, king of Leinster, was defeated in battle with the Red Branch knights whose leader Conall Carnach pursued the king to a place by the Liffey above the fords of Clane and there in single combat slew him. While bearing Mesgedra's head as a trophy Conall was met on the homeward journey to the north by the dead king's wife, Queen Buana, and her maidens. When she is shown the severed head of her husband she reaches out her white arms and dies of grief. With compassion Conall bids his hosts to raise a mound over the body of Buana. In the poem Ferguson blends the story of the queen's death with a lyrical description of the river:

> *Raise too her stone conspicuous far and near;*
> *And let a legend on the long stone tell:*
> *"Behold there lies a tender woman here*
> *Who surely loved a valiant husband well;"*
>
> *Delicious Liffey! from thy bosoming hills*
> *What man who sees thee issuing strong and pure*
> *But with some wistful fresh emotion fills*
> *Akin to nature's own clear temperature?*
>
> *The heath, the fern, the honey fragrant furze*
> *Carpet thy cradling steeps; thy middle flow*
> *Laves lawn and oak wood; o'er thy downward*
> *   course*
> *Laburnums nod and terraced roses blow.*[4]

In this last stanza the topography of the river from its source to the sea has been summarised by the poet.

A few miles to the north is Clongowes Wood College. The nucleus of the school buildings is a much-altered FitzEustace castle which was a border fort of the English Pale. In the 17th century it was purchased by the Brownes who intermarried with the Wogans and in 1813 the castle was sold to the Jesuits. The interior of the school chapel is an example of early 19th century classical work while the new Gothic chapel has Stations of the Cross by Sean Keating and a series of beautiful windows by Michael Healy and Evie Hone. In the nearby historic townlands of Mainham and Rathcoffey are the remains of a medieval church and castle and the mausoleum of the Wogan Brownes. In one of his essays the patriot Thomas Francis

Meagher described this lovely middle flow of the river in words of generous appreciation:

"Oh what a river is that exquisite wild Liffey! How is tumbles; glides away; buries itself darkly in pools of fabulous depths; leaps over rocks, deepens, as it were, thoughtfully under ruins and raths; plunges down into valleys; ripples and whispers under willows, the close leaves of the strawberry and the purple- ivied basements of church tower, country mansion and castle; running the wildest, most ruinous and grandest frolic imaginable until it frowns and grows sulky a little above the King's Bridge of Dublin and, in a turbid thick stream, washes the granite walls of the Quays over which the Four Courts and Customs House rear their stately porticoes and domes".[5]

The Liffey is joined by the Morell river at the village of Straffan. The Catholic church is an attractive old-world edifice and, in the nearby graveyard, are fine yew trees and the remains of ecclesiastical buildings. The parish is named after St. Straffan who ministered there at the end of the 6th century and who was buried at Kill. Straffan House is one of the great mansions of Kildare and, in recent years, huge sums of money have been spent on its restoration and embellishment. It stands beside the river and is surrounded by a meticulously maintained wooded demesne over which it presides in all its grandeur. Adjoining it is the charming residence of Lodge Park which has four detached pavilions. It too stands near the river and has an attractive garden and lawn.

Barberstown Castle, which is in the vicinity, is a rectangular keep with two small towers dating from the 13th century. During the Elizabethan era a large stone dwelling was added. In the early 19th century another wing was included and, at the present time, the owners administer a delightful 15 bed-room hotel in this unique residence.

To the east of the river and beyond the railway line rises the distinctive Hill of Lyons, or Cnoc Liamhain, on the

Dublin-Kildare border. The hill, which commands a view over the plains of the lower Liffey valley, was for centuries the heartland of a sept of the Leinster kings. After the collapse of the native kingdoms the Tyrrells got possession of Lyons and from them it passed, apparently by marriage, to the Aylmers and remained one of their principal seats until the end of the 18th century. It was sold to Nicholas Lawless in 1796. The building of the beautiful Palladian mansion was commenced the following year and completed by his son Valentine, then Lord Cloncurry, about the year 1810. Cloncurry was not only an extensive and keen farmer but was also a traveller on the Grand Tour and a patron of the arts, the fruits of which may be seen in the contents of this elegant house. A well-loved member of the family was Emily Lawless, author and poetess, who lived at Lyons and died in 1913. The estate passed into the possession of University College, Dublin in 1962. It was, until recently, used as an experimental farm dedicated to the advancement of both agriculture and veterinary medicine and the mansion and demesne were preserved by means of sensitive conservation.

The historic village of Newcastle Lyons takes its name from the royal castle and manor which were established here in Norman times. St. Finian had founded a Celtic monastery on this site of which the only relic is a granite cross in the graveyard. The present church of St. Finian is a 15th century nave and chancel edifice with a fine dwelling-and-bell-tower at its western end.

The river continues beside the ancient estate of Killadoon with extensive pastures and fine plantations of timber. The lands were in the possession of several successive owners including the Plunketts of Louth and Conollys of Castletown. The present mansion was erected about 1790 and, since the mid-18th century, most of the lands have been in the possession of the Clements family. In the townland of Ardrass stands the well-preserved 14th century church of St. Patrick which was built in the old Irish manner with a vaulted roof of stones.

Celbridge, or Kildrought, is one of the most historic

places on the Liffey. The early de Hereford castle was built at Castletown and in the 13th century a monastery was founded nearby which was dedicated to St. Wolstan who had then been recently canonised. After the dissolution this property passed to the Allen family who later built the present mansion which is now used as a girls' school. In the grounds may be seen some remains of the medieval priory. Several fine country houses survive in this rich Kildare valley. William Conolly, the speaker of the Irish House of Commons, who became wealthy from dealing in forfeited estates, commenced the building of Castletown House in 1722. This is the largest Palladian mansion in the country and it consists of a centre block of three storeys over a basement joined by two semi-circular colonnades to domestic wings. A splendid hall, imposing reception rooms and elegant plasterwork are features of the mansion while its crowning glory is the long gallery which is the most graceful room in any Irish dwelling. This noble house was purchased and saved in 1967 by the Hon. Desmond Guinness. It is now in the ownership of the Castletown Foundation and is used for education and general cultural purposes. The extensive wooded park slopes gently to the Liffey and, inside the gates, which stand at one end of the main street, are the buildings of Christ Church and a splendid avenue shaded by mature lime trees.

Celbridge Abbey was the home of Esther Van Homrigh and this house will for ever be associated with the memory of Swift and Vanessa. Later the Abbey was acquired by Mr. Justice Marlay the maternal grandfather of Henry Grattan. Speaking later of his determination to fight for an independent parliament Grattan said that it was along the banks of the Liffey, amidst the groves and bowers of Swift and Vanessa, that he grew convinced that he was right. A good view of this lovely building may be obtained from the wooded lawns at the rear near the mill-stream and the bridle-bridge beside the weir. Today the Brothers of St. John of God have a community home in the Abbey and a residential school at Oakley Park, a fine early 18th century stone mansion on the other side of the road.

Donaghcumper is a stately house standing on 100 acres of old manorial parkland stretching to the river. It was enlarged and remodelled in the Tudor-revival style in the early 19th century and contains some fine plasterwork and timbered ceilings. The ruins of the ancient church of Donaghcumper and its graveyard survive and some distance away are the ruins of St. Mochua's church and graveyard. Another notable dwelling is Kildrought House on the Main Street with its garden that descends to the water. In the neighbourhood are the Wonderful Barn, an 18th century conically-shaped building erected for storing corn and the splendid obelisk at the rear of Castletown both of which were erected by William Conolly's widow. It was she too who had the charter school opened after her husband's death. This school, with its fine triple gates, closed in 1972 and the building is now in use as a hotel.

In these fertile plains, when manorial grants of lands were made to Norman knights, castles were erected; so also were corn and tuck mills which were an integral part of such lands. The mills of Kildrought, Donaghcumper and St. Wolstan would appear to date from the settlement of the de Hereford family and their foundation is as old as the manors to which they relate. At Celbridge the mills have been in existence for over seven and a half centuries in the same place. Within a few miles from the town nine mills existed in the 17th century as Lena Boylan has stated in her scholarly article on the mills of Kildrought. After many vicissitudes and interruptions these mills, which stand near the bridge, are being restored as an amenity centre. The first water-mill, which is believed to have been erected in Cappadocia about 70 B.C., is undoubtedly one of the great inventions in history. The contemporary Greek poet, Antipater, wrote an epigram on the event which has been translated as follows:

Ye maids who toil'd so faithful at the mill,
Now cease from work, and from these toils be still;
Sleep now 'till dawn and let the birds with glee
Sing to the ruddy morn on bush and tree;

For what your hands performed so long, so true,
Ceres has charged the water-nymphs to do;
They come, the limpid sisters, to her call,
And on the wheel, with dashing fury, fall;
Impel the axle with a whirling sound,
And make the massy mill-stone reel around,
And bring the floury heaps luxuriant to the
ground.[6]

The area of woodlands in Ireland diminished over the centuries and, by the year 1800, it was estimated that less than two per cent of the land was under trees. Planting was encouraged, however, by legislation and trees were grown by tenants in hedgerows and as ornamental avenues and shelter-belts near dwellings. In Kildare alone almost three million trees were planted the remnants of which still constitute the main sylvan richness of the valley. Splendid examples of oak, ash, beech, sycamore and chestnut may be seen in the estates but many of these are now reaching the end of their life-span and a policy of preservation and renewal has become imperative.

Continuing its journey the river soon flows through the village of Leixlip. There it is joined by the Ryewater or Rige which once formed the historic boundary between the ancient kingdoms of Leinster and Meath. A castle was erected here by Adam de Hereford and the present attractive edifice, which overlooks the confluence of the streams, is an early 18th century mansion but it incorporates two much-altered towers of the early castle. The Church of St. Mary with its medieval tower, the rows of old stone houses, the two bridges and the lovely wooded valley all combine to give special charm to this old water-side village. The distinctive salmon leap, from which the Norse name is derived, became submerged by a hydro-electric scheme and it has been replaced by a fish pass. Further upstream is a beautiful narrow bridge which is a reconstruction of one that dated from the 14th century and which became necessary because of the building of the dam. The level of the old bridge was raised with new materials but it still retains some of the flavour of the *pons antiqua*.

THE RIVER IN DUBLIN

The river now flows directly east and enters County Dublin. The woodlands continue with extensive stretches of pasture and fields of corn or stubble. The first village is Lucan, which was once a fashionable spa, and the river is crossed by an ornate single-span bridge with a high parapet and balustrade near the wide and picturesque weir. Some old buildings, including the stately Protestant church, give character to the place and, immediately to the west, lies the beautiful river-side demesne. In the middle ages the manor of Lucan passed through several hands including the Fitzgeralds and it was eventually acquired by Sir William Sarsfield Mayor of Dublin and ancestor of Patrick Sarsfield, Viscount Tully and Earl of Lucan. Although confiscated under Cromwell the property was later restored to the hero of Ballyneety.

The lands eventually passed by marriage to a Vesey whose son designed the classical Lucan House. This replaced the 16th century tower-house the ruins of which still stand in the demesne next to the old church and graveyard. The mansion, which was later remodelled, has stucco by Michael Stapleton and medallions by Angelica Kauffmann and is now the residence of the Italian ambassador. A few miles to the north is Luttrelstown castle a 19th century castellated mansion incorporating portions of a medieval castle. In the vicinity at Esker are the remains of St. Finian's 15th century parish church and, in the townlands of Pettycanon and Aderrig, respectively, are a ringfort with souterrain and the remains of the old church.

The river now glides peacefully through a beautiful wooded valley with willows drooping and reflected by the long shadows of evening on the water. Having passed by the Strawberry Beds and the weir and gardens of Anna

71

Liffey House and Mill it travels onwards and flows quietly under the bridge at Chapelizod. In the wide and undulating landscape to the south of the river between Lucan and Chapelizod are the estates of St. Edmondsbury, formerly the home of Edmond Sexton Pery, Woodville, Delville, Canon Brook and Hermitage. Palmerston House, which was built by John Hely Hutchinson in 1763, is now incorporated into the Stewart Institution while nearby are the recently-restored remains of Palmerston church which was a small early nave-and-chancel building. To the north are Farmleigh and Knockmaroon Lodge and the splendid extent of the Phoenix Park.

The lands of Chapelizod were part of the property of the Knights Hospitallers of Kilmainham. In 1665 the Duke of Ormond purchased the entire manor for the benefit of the Phoenix Park and the mansion house became the occasional residence of the Lord Lieutenant. The Protestant parish church preserves the belfry of the late-medieval building and the church itself was rebuilt in 1839. The old bell is kept in the porch and is inscribed "I was made for Chapelizard . . . 1720". The bell which is now used is inscribed: "I was cast for Chapelizod . . . 1905". The origin of the name is still a matter of controversy. Some scholars say that it is derived from Isolde the daughter of the Irish king and the tragic heroine of the famous *Tristan and Isolde* legend. Others argue that the name means the chapel of the lazar house and they refer to the former ownership of the land by the Knights Hospitallers of St. John and the spelling of the name in the old documents as Chapel Lizard or Chapel Lazard. It is known that a lazar or leper house did exist formerly in the adjoining manor of Palmerston and this latter place-name is derived from the word meaning a pilgrim who went to the Holy Land and brought back a palm branch in token of the fact.

The village itself has a distinctive old-world character with period houses, a mill-race that passes under antique bridges, the graveyard with its yew trees and the adjoining house which became historic as the scene of Joseph Sheridan Le Fanu's delightful story *The House by the*

Churchyard. In 1982 the main bridge was renamed the Anna Livia bridge to mark the centenary of the birth of James Joyce. After Chapelizod the river banks are often bleak and barren of trees and these miles of placid waters are used by boat clubs for regattas. At Islandbridge tall houses nestle among the trees and present a delicate silhouette against the pale blue of evening while ivy and creepers reach downwards to meet the stream.

From early ages settlers have lived on the rich lands of *Magh Life* beneath remote mountain peaks of timeless beauty and today all of that valley deserves to be protected for posterity. The river flows by well-wooded banks, near holy wells, by ancient ruined churches, splendid historic mansions and through waterside villages. Few capital cities have a stream of pure water so near and so various whether it flows quietly in dark pools or sings its way along over rocks and weirs as it hastens to meet the tide at Islandbridge. The mood of those devious waters has been captured by Joyce in the *Anna Livia Plurabelle* chapter of *Finnegans Wake* in the form of a chattering dialogue across the river by two washerwomen who, as night falls, become a tree and a stone.[7] The action in *Ulysses* was chiefly in the daytime whereas the action in the later work took place at night. "If anyone doesn't understand a passage" he said, "all he need do is read it aloud".[8] His great emphasis was upon the flow of the lines and he cared more for sound and rhythm than for sense.[9] The music of the words and the water was the essence of his theme whether rumbledown rubble or richmond and rare and the closing lines express this idea of movement:

"Can't hear with the waters of. The chittering waters of. Flittering bats, fieldmice bawk talk. . . . Can't hear with bawk of bats, all thim liffeying waters of. Ho, talk save us! My foos won't moos. I feel as old as yonder elm. A tale told of Shaun or Shem? All Livia's daughtersons. Dark hawks hear us. Night! Night! My ho head halls. I feel as heavy as yonder stone. Tell me of John or Shaun? Who were Shem and Shaun the living sons or daughters of? Night now! Tell me, tell me, tell me, elm! Night night! Telmetale of stem or stone. Beside the rivering waters of, hitherandthithering waters of. Night![10]

Joyce said that he conceived the idea of *Finnegans Wake* as the dream of Finn MacCumhaill lying in death beside the river Liffey and watching the history of Ireland and the world flow through his mind like flotsam on the river of life.[11] His work is a rich mosaic of word-music and is the most recent addition to the ancient and continuing Fianna saga.

The river now enters the colonial city below the early church sites of St. Mhaighnann (Kilmainham) St. Columcille and St. Michael and passes near to the Scandinavian lands at Oxmanstown and the old Viking city on the hill. It flows through parishes dedicated to foreign saints such as Audoen, Michan, and Werburgh having passed near the old church and graveyard of St. James. Further downstream it approaches the site of the medieval hospital where pilgrims to the shrine of St. James at Compostela awaited the opportunity to embark near the termination of the present Townsend Street. This street was formerly referred to as Lazar's Hill and is still described in Irish as *Sraid Chnoc na Lobhar*. Flowing under its variable assortment of bridges, buffeted by tide and wind, polluted by the presence of a great city and, having grown weary at the end of its journey, it slides downwards slowly beside the South-wall and mingles with the sea at Poolbeg.

If you stand at the parapet of Ireland's busiest bridge when a promise of spring is in the air and look westwards over the towers and domes of the old city with the evening sky framed by light gray cloud and the spectral blue of the endless horizon streaked by delicate shades of red or pink then the vision of Hy-Brasil returns and bids you to journey onwards for ever and ever and ever towards that wondrous land of the eternal sunset.

NOTES

1. J.P. Griffith, *The Liffey Scheme*, Dublin, 1923.
2. A.P. Smyth, *Celtic Leinster*, Dublin, 1982, p. 49.
3. C. Costello, *Aspects of History*, Co. Kildare, 1988, pp. 9 and 10.
4. T.W. Lyster (editor), *Selected Poetry*, Dublin, 1893.
5. Arthur Griffith (editor), *Meagher of the Sword*, Dublin, 1916.
6. Townlands Index of Ireland, Dublin, 1861 and Baltimore, Maryland, 1984.
7. R. Ellmann, *James Joyce*, London, 1966, p. 575.
8. Ibid., p. 603.
9. Ibid., p. 646.
10. Ibid., p. 557.

SELECT BIBLIOGRAPHY

Killanin and Duignan, *The Shell Guide to Ireland*, London, 1967.

Kilfinane and its Setting

Among the hills of Ireland which stand on the edge of the central plain one of the most attractive and picturesque is the range of the Ballyhoura mountains which rises, in a semi-circular nest-like group, in the quiet south-eastern corner of County Limerick, and which separates the Limerick plains from those of Cork. These hills almost enclose the little market-town of Kilfinane, old-fashioned, unchanging and situated on a broad upland with a superb view from vantage points in, or near, the town of parts of the counties of Tipperary and Cork and, on clear days, the Kerry mountains and the far-away hills of Clare beyond the Shannon and across part of the fertile valley of the Golden Vein.

The town itself is not unlike many others in Ireland except for its unique site and setting. Although an inhabited centre at least since Homeric times, it is quiet with the quietness of a town at the end of the trail, built as it is largely in a *cul-de-sac*, by-passed by the main roads and standing as a kind of tiny capital of that beautiful border country of hills, glens and streams which forms the southern boundary of the barony of Coshlea and which, like the kingdom of Piedmont in Italy, is named from its position at the foot of the mountains. A fine view of this landscape may be had from the train on the journey between Kilmallock and Knocklong.

In a vague way Kilfinane has the aspect of a German village, set as it is in the pine and fir trees of the state forest and, through whose streets, tiny rivulets of water ran over their cobbled beds which, though now mostly covered in, reminded one of Freiburg in the Black Forest of Baden while, nearby, is the small settlement of Palatines, the descendants of some of those who came to Ireland as refugees from the wars of Louis XIV. Having been first settled at Rathkeale, colonies went to Adare, Pallaskenry, Kilfinane and the small village of Ballyorgan. Within the present generation, names such as Bovenizer, Fitzelle, Steepe and Shumacher gave a slightly foreign flavour to the parish and disclosed the Germanic origin of these settlers from the Palatinate, commemorated by the name of Palatines' Rock near their homesteads in the townland of Ballyriggin.

The town, and much of the adjoining property, was owned by the Oliver family of whom the Gascoignes were a branch. Many of the houses were built by them including some solid stone dwellings near the centre and the Georgian building of the former hotel, and it was they too who flagged the footpaths with slabs of even slate-stone which lasted down to recent years until replaced by a modern concrete surface. Not far from the town are the, now ruined, oatmeal mills where the great wheel was once turned by the waters of the Lúbach. Nearby was the old-fashioned Mill House, with its monkey tree embosomed in beautiful deciduous woods which gave a sedate and Victorian appearance to this portion of the district while, at the crossroads, is the artistically conceived grotto to Our Lady and the head weir of the river. Apparently other mills were situate in the last century at Sunville two miles to the west and adjoining the historic hill of Ardpatrick.

In the centre is the square, now largely occupied by a statue of the Sacred Heart and its shrine, enclosed by walls and decorated by shrubs, trees and beds of flowers. There too is the cistern with its flow of water and old disused gas standard while immediately to the rear, is the spacious market-house where, as related in his journal, John Wesley preached to the Palatines during his Irish journey and which building, of fine stone construction, was substantially repaired in 1836.

Among the older houses in the neighbourhood are Spring Lodge, Brookville Cottage, Spa Hill and Glen-Dove House with their lawns and laurel groves, their old trees and cobbled yards while the Glebe House or Rectory was built in 1813 and is a fine country house with a spacious fruit and vegetable garden. Not far away was the primary school for boys with its large Romanesque windows facing the sun and with maps of far-away places and a tiny science and natural-history laboratory which hold many happy memories for me. At the other end of the town a solid stone bridewell or gaol was also built in the last century consisting of two days rooms, two yards and four cells but this has long since been used for residential purposes while, near the square, was the pound where straying animals were confined. A century ago, Quarter Sessions were held in the town and later removed to Bruff. Now, a District Court only is held in these smaller places.

There too are the old farmhouses of The Priory and Ashbrook situate, respectively, in a garden and a lawn, the later covered with ivy and protected from the winds by its sycamore and beech trees. St. Andrew's Villa, called after the patron saint of the parish, formerly the house of a boys' secondary school and the home of the classical teacher, is now a guest-house. In the town itself the shops have the traditional timber fronts often with ornamental carvings in wood while, here and there, the nature of the commodities sold is displayed with signs and notices by some of the merchants.

The Protestant church, now enclosed by high walls and mature trees, was rebuilt in 1760 and restored in later years. The fabric is mainly of sandstone while the spire is crowned by the proverbial weather-cock. In the interior is some fine Gothic vaulting on stout limestone pillars. Some marble plaques commemorate members of the Oliver family and the widow of the Reverend George Wren who was rector of the parish for forty years. A stained-glass window showing the ascent of Our Lord into heaven was erected by parishioners and friends to his memory while another window, containing writings from the Scriptures, commemorates Joseph Wiggins who was the clerk and schoolmaster at Kilfinane for forty eight years. A bell used for 150 years in the old church is preserved near the nave.

The names appearing on the tombs and head-stones in the surrounding churchyard provide an interesting record of families belonging to the religious minority who lived in the parish in the past century. They include Bailey, Brew-Hannan, Ellard, Flood-Davin, Gifford, Harris, Hinchy, Low, Mee, Naylor, Oliver, Read, Sherwood, Shumacher, Stanley and Steepe. The Protestant parish is now united with others in the neighbourhood and I can recall, from a few generations back, the sharp and lengthy peals of the bell for the Sunday afternoon service attended by members of the Church of Ireland including some Palatine families in the area.

The Catholic church is of more recent date and is built on the edge of a hill overlooking the plains to the north. Like the adjoining presbytery it is built of the beautiful old red sandstone which prevails in the district. In the baptistery is a modern fresco by Father Aengus Buckley O.P., depicting the baptism of Christ and in the right transept is the grave of my grand-uncle who was parish priest at the time the church was built towards the end of the last century and to whose memory the west window of stained-glass, with the figures of the four Evangelists, was donated. In the apse, behind the attractive marble altar, is some good stained-glass, and at a side chapel are two beautiful little windows of Our Lady of Perpetual Succour and Good Counsel before which the silver lamp was sometimes lighted. Around the church are pleasant lawns, gravelled paths and trees, while the convent of the Sisters of Charity of St. Paul the Apostle and primary, secondary and vocational schools lend a monastic atmosphere to this most northerly point of the town.

The countryside around Kilfinane is a land of colour and beauty not only in its physical form and appearance but in its very place-names. It is a land of many quiet country roads coming over the hills or through the valleys which indicate its importance as an early inhabited centre. Two of them were formerly passes, one leading to Mitchelstown by the wood-road and the bridge or viaduct of Barrabunocka *under* which the road continues on the way

79

to Darragh, formerly the site of a great oak forest and now through a countryside beautifully planted with the formal outline of pine woods. At the junction of the counties is the bridge of Ahaphúca or the ford of the fairies.

The other road leads to Doneraile by way of Ardpatrick and the wild and lonely landscape of Glenanaar, the scene of Canon Sheehan's novel of that name. In the area is the frowning mass of Blackrock and the smaller Blackhill topped by its ring fort and, at its foot, the two sandstone quarries of the district. There too is the Green Wood now splendidly restored after it cutting during the war and, further on, the pass of Red Chair or Red Gap where Cork and Limerick meet while, nearer home, is the townland of Ballyroe so called from the colour of the prevailing red sandstone of the hills.

To the east is Slieve Reagh (Sliabh Riabhach), gentle on the Limerick side and partly cultivated with woodland, rough pasture and fields while the eastern slope consists of dark and hostile cliffs like a great fortress carved by natural forces for the protection of the plains which stretch to the north along the valleys of the Lúbach, the Morningstar and the Camoge rivers in the counties of Limerick and Tipperary. In the hills the golden blaze of gorse in spring was often a close rival to the burning of the furze themselves to provide sweeter grass in summer while, in later months, the rich harvest of whortleberries in the nearby plantation occupied many a useful hour of our childhood vacations.

Here also is a land of wells and streams. There is Tobar Finan called after the local saint of early christian days (probably Saint Finan Lobhar, or the Leper, associated with Swords and Aghadoe) and which, cold and crystal clear, thrusts its waters through a bed of cress as a tiny tributary of the Lúbach, and there is Lady's Well near the woods, a place of pilgrimage surrounded by its grove and objects of piety. Some miles away near Emlygrennan is the well of Saint Molua, which is the object of a pattern early in August, while, adjoining the town, is Tobar More quiet and peaceful as is fitting for a well surrounded on all sides by the fertile fields of the valley.

In the hills too several tiny brooks and streams have their birth and which sing their way through many a wild romantic glen with all the gay abandonment of youth. One of these streams is the Noneen near the hamlet of Glenosheen where Patrick Weston Joyce the historian and Robert Dwyer Joyce the poet were born. It flows through a land of legend adjoining the mountain peak of Seefin — the resting place of Finn — and not far from Leaba Oscar at Mountrussell where his grandson lies buried in mythical memory under the corbelled stones of a megalithic tomb. The stream then passes under Gotoon bridge near Ballingaddy so called from the legend of the black robber who dwelt in this area and who gave his name to the Cross of Black where the roads from Ardpatrick and Kilfinane unite about half-way from Kilmallock.

This district preserves the names of three generations of the Fianna, a military order which attained its greatest eminence in the third century during the reign of Cormac Mac Airt and under the leadership of Finn. Oisin was his son and Oscar his grandson. They were the last heroes of pagan Ireland who, before they died, bequeathed their names to the well-marked features of this lonely valley of the Ballyhouras while the adjoining hill of Ardpatrick, with its ruin-covered slopes, perpetuates the name of the Apostle of Christianity.

The plains to the north were one of the favourite hunting grounds of the ancient Irish. Wild deer and ox seem to have abounded in them and then, as now, the pleasures of the chase were a human feature of the area. In the Book of Glendalough occurs a conversation between Cuchullin of the Red Branch knights and his charioteer Leagh. Both are standing on the hill of Knockainy north of Kilmallock and Cuchullin is pointing out to his attendant the chief features of the country which they see from the summit. The passage is as follows: "Tell me my charioteer Leagh dost thou know in what country we now are?" "I know it not, indeed," replied the charioteer. "I know it well" said Cuchullin. "The mountain lying to the south is Ceann

Abrat Sleibhi Cain (now Slieve Reagh). Those mountains to the north are Sleibhte Eibhlinn (now Slieve Phelim). That bright sheet of water which thou seest is the lake of Limerick; the hill on which we stand is called Druim Collcaille which is also called Aine Cliach. It is situated in the territory of Deise beag."

To the south and east of the town, and coming from a variety of sources, rises the Lúbach which, true to its name, twists and winds its way through the valleys in a manner very like the Mosel, its larger cousin in Germany, and which fertilize and drain, respectively, part of the rich meadows of Desmond in Limerick and the ancient vineyards of Berncastel and Cochem near the wooded hills of the Rhenish-Palatinate.

Situate in a countryside of height and hollow the town has several pleasant country walks with many stone bridges crossing the tributary brooks of the Lúbach. There is the top road to Ballinlina and Abbey cemetery near the village of Ballyorgan skirting the demesne of Clonodfoy with smaller tracks giving an easy ascent of Corrig and the hills beyond. There too is a complex of ways leading, by the well-road and the former cheese factory, to Moorstown or to Palatine hill and Ruppulagh. A straight road leads to Ardpatrick by way of Mortlestown and Sunville House — formerly the residence of the Godsall family — passing the pond at Murrin's cross, still shaded by its ash tree, while an easy descent to the lowlands crosses the bridge at Ballinanima, the ancestral home of my maternal kinsmen.

For mountain walks a convenient way is to Beann and Gooseberry hill from the Ballinlina road while, to the east, the splendid view from Slieve Reagh towards the Galtees over the rich lands of Ormond is matched only by the sight from Seefin mountain when so much of Munster is at your feet and the watershed is crossed, with views towards the historic valleys of the Awbeg and the Funsion near Kildorrery, and Kilcolman Castle where Spenser wrote many of the silver stanzas of *The Faerie Queene* while, further afield, are the Knockmealdowns and the Nagles mountains of central Cork. It is a land which reflects all the varied moods of the changing seasons. In late spring it is a carpet of colour while, with frost, the peaks stand out in splendour or take on a mystical beauty when shrouded by October mists or caressed by the autumn dew and, when snow falls thick, it is easy to recall the loveliness of an Alpine pass. In early summer the warm breezes play hide-and-seek among the meadows on the high slopes changing the grass into a silken pattern of endless variety.

Kilfinane has its history as well as its legends although never as important in medieval and later days as Kilmallock. The owners of the town and its rents included Walter Purcell in 1350 and Garrett MacThomas in 1588. In 1590 Edmund FitzGibbon, the White Knight, was granted the head rent of the town and, in 1657, Kilfinane was described as a place "where there is a good castle, the walls of a church and an Irish Downe." This latter phrase describes the dun or fort, always referred to locally as the moat of Kilfinane. In the extracts from the *Journal* of Thomas Dinely, which give an account of his visit to Ireland during the reign of Charles II, the author states that a mountain, which formed part of the estate of Clonodfoy, split asunder, about February 1680, and sent forth a river of water.

Some miles to the west is the vividly green hill of Ardpatrick which is said to have been the most southerly point of St. Patrick's journey. Here he built a church which developed into a monastery, the ruins of which may still be seen as well as the stump of a round tower which, on such a site, must have been one of the finest in the Ireland of its day. Nearby is a deep well and a graveyard ancient and new. In olden times this height was known as the hill of the Fianna where the valley of Glenosheen opens into the southern lowlands of County Limerick and it was here that Celsus, Archbishop of Armagh, died in 1129. It is said that the monastery possessed a peal of five bells of marvellous beauty which were concealed at the time of the suppression and the story is told that, at Christmas and Easter, the melody of the bells rings out at midnight startling the people with tones of the most exquisite music.

On his return from Tirnanog (the land of the young) in Christian days Oisin, the bard and hero of the Ossianic legends, is represented in one of the stories, as saying with nostalgia, to Saint Patrick: "Hateful to me is the sound of the bells and the howling of thy lean clerics. There is no joy in your strait cells, no pleasant music. Oh! for one hour with the Fianna whom I knew. I swear to thee O lean cleric that better was one day with Finn and his heroes than a thousand years of the kingdom of heaven."!

In the town are the extensive ruins of an ancient church which are still surrounded by a burial ground. On the tombstones, or in the surrounding countryside, among the many names, obviously representing Gaelic and Hiberno-Norman stock, appear the rather uncommon surnames of Derham, Egleston, England, Fettin, Hardacre, Lipsett, Lundon, MacCreery, Thornhill, Welstead and Young. Near these ancient church ruins are the remains of the castle which is believed to have been built by the Roches and destroyed in Cromwellian days. The surviving portion of the castle shows that it had massively thick walls and was built of red sandstone blocks.

The northern slopes of the hills, thickly covered with forest trees, formed the woods of Kilquaig and were frequently mentioned in the records of the 16th century. They were also referred to as Kylemore (the great wood), and they played an important part in the tragic Desmond rebellion when the gallant James Fitzmaurice FitzGerald and, later, the Earl of Desmond sheltered here from the army of the Lord President of Munster stationed at Kilmallock. These woods connected the fastnesses of Aherlow with the strong defensive position of Upper Connelloe and afforded a safe passage from one to the other and a hiding place for Gael and Norman with the declining fortunes of their power. Several battles were fought in the woods in ancient days and, in the Annals of the Four Masters, are found many references to them and to this remote and secluded portion of the county. The most important early historical event connected with the district is the murder of Mahon, King of Munster, and brother of Brian Boru.

At the foot of Slieve Reagh in the townland of Cush lies a unique complex of earthworks containing pre-Christian dwellings and a burial ground which formed the subject matter of an extensive excavation in 1934 and 1935 while other forts exist also at Cush and the adjoining townlands of Ballinvreena and Glenbrohane. The excavation provided evidence of an agricultural community that inhabited the site during the greater part of the last millennium B.C. and the beginning of our era. It gave the earliest definite date yet available for ring-forts and souterrains which are known to have been constructed well into medieval times. In his report the late Professor O'Riordan, who conducted the excavations, stated that, in addition, ancient fields and fences were discovered nearby and the importance of this, almost the first to be noted in Ireland, lay in the fact that it proved the essential similarity of the present-day field system and the pre-historic one and demonstrated the basic continuance of Irish farming to the present day.

This fact arose from the historic continuity in Ireland of an agricultural arrangement which, in Britain, was interrupted by the introduction, with the Saxons, or, perhaps with the Romans, of one which was very different. The Irish idea of square of rectangular fields was introduced in pre-historic times into both countries but was superseded in southern Britain, after the Anglo-Saxon invasions, by the strip system which continued throughout medieval times. In Ireland, there was no break in the continuity of the early arrangement. Hence while many changes of boundaries took place, resulting in the alteration of the size of fields, the present-day system is the direct descendant of the ancient one and, only by the combination of favourable circumstances, as at Cush, can the two be distinguished.

South from Moorestown is the conspicuous, though small, wood of Ballyriggin on the slope of a hill consisting of mature Scotch Fir trees said to have been planted on the site of an ancient place of burial while, here and there, one finds remains of stones and mounds which mark a place of ancient habitation and importance. Immediately behind the town is the splendid ringed fort, which is perhaps the largest of its kind in the county. It consists of a huge earthen mound sixty feet in diameter at the base and sloping towards the summit where, at the widest part, it is twenty-four feet across. It rises about forty feet above the trench and is partly encircled by ramparts fourteen feet high. They are still in tolerable preservation on the west side and some scholars consider the structure to have been erected, or restored, by Brian Boru.

Not far south of the town is Corrig hill, on the western slope of which is a great bulk of coarse conglomerate rock called the corrigeens near the cross-roads of that name. It is different from the prevailing red sandstone of the district and different also from the limestone of the plains and is possibly of volcanic origin, or caused by the intense pressure of soil and shale during the passing of the ice age. To the west the Greenwood, near Ardpatrick, overlooks the splendid demesne of Castle Oliver, or Clonodfoy, which was successively occupied by the Roches and the Fitzharrises and, after Cromwell, by the Olivers and the Trenches.

In the castle Maria Dolores Gilbert (1818-1861), better known as Lola Montez, is said to have been born. Her father, Edward Gilbert, an ensign in the 44th foot, died of cholera in India in 1825, having been married to a Miss Oliver of the Castle who had Spanish blood and who, after her husband's death, married a Captain Craigie. Having been instructed in dancing for four months and, after a short visit to Spain, Lola made her debut in London but was badly received. She had considerable success, however, as a Spanish dancer in Berlin and Dresden and went to Paris, Warsaw and to St. Petersburg where she was welcomed warmly by the Czar and showered with presents. In 1847 she appeared as a dancer in Munich, completely captivated the old king of Bavaria, Ludwig I, and exercised a strong fascination over the ministers. Eventually in March 1848, with the insurrection, she was banished from the kingdom and the monarch was forced to abdicate. After further adventures in America and Australia she devoted the latter years of her life to charitable work and died, in New York, in 1861.

The early castles are long since in ruins and a large mansion of red sandstone was erected nearby in the first half of the last century. The estate, which occupies a wide valley between the hills, was divided by the Land Commission a few generations ago but the mansion survives with a few hundred acres surrounded by woodlands. In the fruitful months the view from the mountain road is delightful and the landscape has all the charms of Killarney with much better air, lacking only the lakes and the whimsical legends. It lies in the civil parish of Particles and may have been part of the lands of the White Knights. In 1657 the castle was described as "an old ruined stone house and bawn" held by the Fitzharris family and which was later granted to Robert Oliver. One of the best early descriptions of this countryside appears in Arthur Young's *Tour in Ireland* (1776-1779).

An interesting an human story of the Oliver family towards the end of the 18th or beginning of the 19th century relates to the maternal ancestors of the Joyces of Glenosheen, historian and poet. Their maternal grandfather was John O'Dwyer of Glendara who became acquainted with a Mary Rosaleen Weston at the dancing school in Kilfinane and became fascinated by her charm and beauty. She was a daughter of Major Weston of Ballinacurra-Weston near Limerick. They married privately and O'Dwyer took his wife to live amongst his own people. Different in class and in creed, the Westons repudiated the marriage of their daughter and heiress with an Irish Papist. Under the penal laws which were still in force the gallant O'Dwyer might well have been hanged if the Westons sought the full rigour of the law. Captain Oliver of the castle, however, exercised his influence with Major Weston to save O'Dwyer who was his neighbour and who was popular as well. He arranged a meeting between the pair and the major was so highly pleased with the fine appearance and fascinating manners of his son-in-law that he acknowledged the marriage. A daughter, Elizabeth, married Garret Joyce of Glenosheen. They were the parents of Parick Weston Joyce the local historian and Robert Dwyer Joyce one of the poets of the legends of Ireland. A romantic story from a very romantic land!

The remaining area of the estate is still intensively cultivated and the demesne with its residence represents today an epitome of the history of land ownership in large areas of Ireland. In ancient times, the valley was, for the most part, primeval forest and probably within the territory of Gaelic chieftains and their vassals. Later Hiberno-Norman families possessed it and then it passed to the favourites of Cromwell until today, divided and partly restored to the descendants of the early owners, the sturdy Victorian dwelling-house, with its battlements and spires and its fine stone gateways, surrounded by lawns and ancient trees, represents the continuity of solid building which started with the medieval castle of the early Norman knights.

Behind it all stand the Galtees, the loveliest of our inland mountains, rising in spear-like shapes towards the sky, crowned often by mists and passing clouds and, sometimes, by the glistening white of winter or the rose-pink colours of sunset on the snow. Always the little lakes are dwelling there high up among the ancient undisturbed stillness of the peaks and whispering their lonely story to the barren shores, often with the breath of absolute silence in the air.

If one is lucky in the day the view from Galtymore is superb. There she stands in undisputed reign over the great fertile valleys of Munster with the lesser hills crouching around her like handmaidens paying homage to their queen. Here and there the remnants of some ancient woods blend pleasantly with the more formal outline of the newly-planted pine and fir trees and, at times, one hears the song of the tiny brooks as they gurgle their way merrily along over the rocky beds as though in great haste to reach their maturity in the lowland streams and their final fulfilment in the sea. With it, too, comes a sense of achievement after the long climb up and, as part of the reward, come the joys of the journey down. With the west wind blowing softly in your face and the sigh and the scent of the heather all around, with the grouse rising at your feet and, above, the plaintive cry of the curlew as he seeks out his feeding grounds by the sea then, indeed, one becomes possessed by a great happiness and sometimes, even if only for a few brief moments, one comes very near to Nirvana. And I can recall a day late in February, on another beautiful mountain, as I trudged slowly upwards knee-deep in snow, seeing, for a brief spell, the splendid outline of two male deer. With their heads erect and their antlers back they seemed to sense the presence of an intruder in their desert kingdom and then they were gone leaving me alone to ponder upon that moment of unique beauty and to file it fondly away among the archives of my memory.

Some German cities in 1952

It was on a sunny autumn afternoon that I arrived in the ancient town of Aachen which was a favourite residence of Charlemagne and which lies in a fertile basin surrounded by gently-sloping hills. It was a Sunday afternoon and the town was gay as European cities are wont to be on the Sabbath. My steps naturally turned towards the cathedral, for the Münster of Aachen is one of the most famous of the Sacred buildings of Europe. It consists of two distinct parts in different styles. The earlier part, erected by Charlemagne, is a beautiful example of the Byzantine style, being an octagon copied from S. Vitale at Ravenna with a lofty exquisite roof of the 17th century and several adjoining chapels, while the Gothic choir, remarkable for its light and elegant proportions, possesses enormous windows filled with richly-coloured stained glass executed at Cologne and Aachen itself.

Alone among the important historical monuments of the city the cathedral escaped the war with but relatively slight damage while most of the other churches were either largely destroyed or burnt out and the 14th century Rathhaus was very severely damaged in the air-raids. For all that, it was pleasant in the centre of the town where the crowds had gathered. Many of the buildings were either being rebuilt or had not been destroyed and the general air was one of brightness and even prosperity, while the cafés and restaurants were full and sometimes lively with the sound of music as the people chatted in pleasant surroundings and to the strains of German waltzes.

In contrast to many of the larger German cities the

centre of Hamburg did not appear severely destroyed although much of the residential area was in ruins or had been recently restored. Unquestionably the great attraction of the city is the Alster — a beautiful sheet of water bounded by palatial hotels and houses and by a fine park and promenades. It was very cheerful in the autumn sunshine with launches and boats plying across the lake and the two open-air cafés near the water filled with people while the copper roofs or spires of some of the public buildings and churches, so familiar in the old Hansa towns of Germany, presented an attractive sky-line. The magnificent city hall with its saloons and rooms richly decorated with tapestries and wood- carving, and which is also the parliament house of the state of Hamburg, fortunately escaped damage while the museums had on the whole fared very well and their contents were for the greater part safe. The buildings of the Hansa university were rather extensively damaged but had been restored while, unfortunately, the only two churches which survived the great fire in the middle of the last century, were gravely damaged by the bombing. The city was the centre of a flower exhibition in the summer and, at night, the park was the centre of open-air concerts while two restaurants with music and dancing, added the last necessary touch of gaiety to an already lovely park.

The centre of Bremen appeared to be more destroyed than the other Hansa towns of the Baltic but the city was particularly fortunate in that its two most famous squares, with their precious buildings, had survived. The intimate market-place with its lovely town hall, its famed statue of Roland and its chamber of commerce is much the same today as it had been since the spacious days of the Hanseatic League although the modern building of the Exchange nearby was largely destroyed by the bombs. The fine Romanesque cathedral and the old Liebfrauenkirche, which adjoins the market, also survived intact. It is the Rathhaus, however, which gives such charm to this area of the *Altstadt*. A Gothic and Renaissance building, with its Doric columns and richly-decorated bow-window handsome gable and green copper roof, it has few equals among the town halls of Northern Europe and has come down to us through the centuries untouched by anything save time. In the interior is the Great Hall with its stained glass, its portraits of the emperors and its models of old ships which immediately impress the visitor with the true atmosphere of this ancient and historic port of the Baltic.

Lübeck, however, possesses most of the medieval relics of these three Hanseatic towns of the Empire. The city had one air raid during the war and most of it has survived though some of the finest examples of merchants' houses of the late Gothic and Renaissance periods had disappeared and the more important of the famous brick churchs, including the cathedral and the Marienkirche, suffered grave damage. The Rathhaus, a Gothic brick building with huge gables and quaint spires and, architecturally, one of the most important buildings in Germany, was largely intact as were the two medieval brick gateways which give such character to the town.

After an all-night train journey I reached the University town of Göttingen which had come through the war almost unscathed and where many of the houses bear inscriptions to the memory of distinguished scholars and students such as the brothers Grimm, the German jurist Savigny and the poet Longfellow. Göttingen was very attractive in the early morning of a warm autumn day and in the quiet old-world streets were many half-timbered houses, scarcely altered since the middle ages, which blended gracefully with the changing style of later centuries. It was pleasant indeed to linger for a while in this old Lower-Saxon town before reaching the beautiful valley of the Lahn and its historic towns of Marburg, Wetzlar, Limburg and the watering place of Bad Ems, all of which had survived with little damage from the war. If Göttingen was a pleasant mixture of the old and the new, the ancient heart of Marburg proved to be a perfect picture of a medieval city charmingly situated in a semicircle round the precipitous Schlossberg and on the quiet waters of the Lahn. It too has a university dating from the 16th century and, in addition, the presence of the beautiful church of St. Elizabeth in the early Gothic style, the ancient castle of the princes of Hesse high above the town, and the market-place with its town hall, its fountain and half-timbered houses give a character to Marburg which is particularly captivating even when compared with the traditional beauty of the surviving towns of medieval Germany. This church not merely shelters the remains of St. Elizabeth but also those of Frederick the Great* and Hindenburg and, in the extensive and well-preserved schloss may still be seen the room where Luther, Zwingli, Melanchthon and others met, at the invitation of Philip of Hesse, to seek an adjustment of their differences regarding the Eucharist.

It is not far down the valley to Wetzlar, a quiet little city, which presents such a strange contrast to its one-time dignity as legal capital of the Holy Roman Empire and which must for ever be associated with Goethe and with his world-famed story *The Sorrows of Werther*. To this little capital Goethe came to complete his legal studies by experience in the Imperial Court of Justice whose building with the Imperial eagle may still be seen, as also may the house in the Schiller-Platz where the tragic death of Werther occurred. Many half-timbered houses survive in the market-place with its fountain and flowers and the memories of the poet hang heavily over the town as they do over the nearby villages of Garbenheim and Volpertshausen so intimately associated with the Wetzlar days of Goethe.

The Lahn flows pleasantly through the well-wooded valley passing old towns with their towers and castles until eventually Limburg is reached about half way from the Rhine. The pride of Limburg is the vast cathedral, with its seven towers, which rises conspicuously above the river and forms a well-known landmark for miles around. The

---

*In 1952 the remains of Frederick were removed from Marburg to Burg Hechingen near Stuttgart and, on the 18th August 1991, they were reinterred in the grounds of Schloss Sanssouci in Potsdam.

interior, however, does not equal the glory of the outside partly due to over restoration and to necessary preservation of the fabric of one of Germany's oldest and best-loved churches. Beneath the building the town itself, with its ancient bridge and many picturesque half-timbered houses, lies along the Lahn and forms a pleasant example of one of the surviving cathedral towns of Germany.

From Limburg to the Rhine near Coblenz was a pleasant journey down the valley with its meadows and, at times, its steep heights rising from the water and always rich with pine woods. Here and there towns like Diez and Nassau were reached with their schloss or the ruins of some ancient burg crowning the adjacent hilltops until finally the Lahn mingled with the Rhine above Coblenz. Coblenz itself was heavily bombed during the war and the fact that so many of the essential features of the city have survived was a pleasant surprise when the general ruin of the centre of the town was examined. Few places on the Rhine can vie with the city in beauty of situation, standing as it does at the junction of two of the most picturesque rivers in Europe for it is here that the Mosel joins the great river and lovely views may be had in every direction not merely from the famous Rhine Promenade, which had retained its charm, but from the top of the fortress of Ehrenbreitstein which rises on a precipitous rock on the opposite side of the river. The 18th century palace, the Mosel bridge, the ancient burg and some of the churches had survived, while, in particular, the magnificent 12th century church of St. Castor, although damaged a little, had again regained its ancient beauty.

From the Rhine a journey into Bavaria can best be made up the beautiful valley of the Main with its particularly placid waters and with rich meadows and forests as the river winds its way slowly by ancient undamagd towns like Miltenberg and Wertheim through the heart of Franconia. But not all the cities of the Main had come through the war so well for one of its most beautiful treasures — St. Kilian's ancient city of Würzburg — suffered heavy ruin in a bombing attack towards the end. The 12th century cathedral, the vast and beautiful palace, the Marienkapelle in the market-place, the ancient fortress of Marienberg and much of the centre of the town suffered severe damage in the raid. However it is more pleasant to catalogue the treasures that had remained and to linger on the fact that, while the loss was undoubtedly great, important parts of the damaged buildings had survived and, in my view, the greater part of the town was capable of ultimate restoration.

Würzburg remains, as it always has been, a city of fountains. Near the station, in the palace courtyard, and before the Rathhaus are three of the most beautiful whose waters add their artisitic pattern to a rich and ancient background. A lucky survivor was the principal staircase of the Residenz, an imposing and beautiful structure in the centre of the palace adorned with a fresco by Tiepolo representing Olympus and the four quarters of the globe. This unique staircase and the splendid central saloons have retained their glories though both wings of the building were but empty shells while the outer walls were everywhere standing. The cathedral was out of bounds to the traveller as restoration work proceeded with feverish activity as it did also at the lovely Marienkapelle in the Markt though, in the latter case, the visitor was free to enter to see the progress of the work which could be executed with perfection as the beautiful portal and slender tower survived as also had the outline of the fine baroque house adjoining which provides much of the personality of the market-place.

A climb up to the hill, opposite the city, on which stands the ancient fortress, was well worth the trouble for the Marienberg castle, although somewhat shattered in parts since the war, had retained much of its old dignity and contains a fine museum. The view too from the terrace was superb. Below winds the broad and lazy river spanned by the old and undamaged bridge adorned with statues of saints, including Kilian and Charlemagne, while the city itself rises up the gentle slopes beyond. With its red roofs and the outline of its fine buildings including the university, Julius Hospital, town hall and the Neumünster Church, the town appeared unscathed until on closer inspection ragged gaps in the fabric appeared noticeable, although they were then much less than the sum total of solid buildings of the city.

It was pleasant to enter the town of Bamberg, also in Franconia, for here was a city with a rather similar history to Würzburg but which had the singular good fortune to survive intact. About half the town is built upon a row of small hills, the highest point of which is crowned with several churches, while the fine Rathhaus is built on a bridge and standing, with an independent air, between the upper and lower parts of the town. Undoubtedly the glory of Bamberg is the cathedral which, with the adjoining old and new palaces, form one of the finest groups of buildings of its kind in Europe. The cathedral was founded by the Emperor Henry II in the 11th century but dates, in its present form, from the 12th century. It is the four towers which give the exterior its character while, in the interior, in the centre of the nave, is the sarcophagus of the founder and his consort Cunigunde executed in stone by Riemenschneider the most distinguished sculptor of his time in Germany. Beautifully-carved reliefs adorn the sides. An unusual feature of the building is its two choirs and this, together with the elegant purity of style, the presence of many fine statues, including the famous Domreiter or equestrian statue near St. George's choir, and the four beautiful doorways make the Dom of Bamberg the loveliest cathedral in all Bavaria with the possible exception of that at Regensburg.

On the way to that city of the Danube, a call to Coburg and Bayreuth was not wasted. With the exception of some destruction to a part of the latter town both have survived unharmed. The former town, as one of the residences of the Dukes of Saxe — Coburg — Gotha and with a statue of Prince Albert in the market-place, boasts of a number of handsome buildings including the spacious Moritzkirche, the ducal palace and the theatre but it is the splendid castle of Coburg, on a hill above the town and approached through a lovely park, that provides such character and historical significance to the place. This great and ancient palace, restored and fitted up as a museum, is a fine example of a German residential castle towering above the little principality and commanding the entire district. Bayreuth itself, with its memories of Wagner, and its handsome outline and buildings, and, in particular, the charming yet small 18th century Opera House is yet another of those small ducal cities with which Germany, and Bavaria in particular, is so richly endowed.

Regensburg, beautifully situated at the confluence of the Danube and the Regen, was for centuries the most prosperous city in the south of Germany. At an early period it was a free town of the Empire and for over a century was the permanent seat of the Imperial Diet. Some of the numerous medieval houses still retain crests of their former owners especially those in the Street of the Ambassadors where residences of several ambassadors to the Diet were situated. Regensburg today has acquired a new distinction for it ranks probably with Heidelberg as one of the largest cities of Germany which came through the war with only the slightest damage. Like Bamberg its finest building is the famed cathedral. A splendid Gothic edifice, it resembles that of Strasbourg while its chief external features are the twin spires and a beautiful facade with the main portal and a triangular portico of the 15th century. Many treasures adorn the interior from a monument in bronze erected in the nave to the smaller monuments along the sides of the aisles. Other noteworthy treasures include the five side altars with handsome Gothic canopies, the Gothic pulpit of the 15th century, the splendid silver high-altar presented in the 18th century by Prince-Bishop Count Fugger and the elegant ciborium with numerous statuettes executed in the 15th century.

In addition to many old churches, including the lovely unspoilt church of St. James in the purest Romanesque style, Regensburg can boast of the Rathhaus where the Imperial Diet held its meetings and which, with its elegant bow-window and handsome portal as well as its Imperial

Hall and rich historic furnishings, is well worthy of the ancient importance of the city. Not far away is the famous Walhalla, a German Temple of Fame founded by King Ludwig in 1830 as a home for the busts of celebrated Germans who were deemed worthy by the illustrious founder to grace his hall of the chosen.

Three almost-perfect towns grace the landscape of Middle Franconia. Complete with medieval walls, old half-timbered houses and an atmosphere quite unspoilt, Rothenburg, Dinkelsbühl and Nördlingen have changed but little since the Thirty Years War so happily passed them by with the exception of the damage, though relatively small, which came to Rothenburg in 1945. These towns are too well known to need a lengthy description but, while it is true that Rothenburg is the most famous and the most wealthy artistically of the three, nevertheless the old Imperial town of Dinkelsbühl, surrounded by walls and towers and sleeping peacefully on the quiet waters of the Wörnitz with an unparalleled series of high-pitched roofs, wide eaves and dormer windows, with a great profusion of scarlet geraniums and the changing shadows of an autumn day, will always remain for me the most perfect little city in all of Germany and, perhaps, in all the world.

The White Knights and their Kinsmen

Among the more historically important people who rose to power in Europe in the early middle ages were the Normans, the descendants of the raiding Vikings of earlier centuries. Having settled in the fertile fields and orchards of Normandy they set out on campaigns of conquest over great areas of Europe, even as far afield as Sicily. They conquered England in 1066 and soon fine buildings and cities arose in every part of that kingdom, castles, churches and monasteries taking pride of place.

In 1169, during the reign of Henry II, the invasion of Ireland was commenced under the pretext of an invitation from Dermot, king of Leinster, and a rather ineffecutal Bull of Pope Adrian, the Englishman. Futher to justify the invasion of the smaller island the ambitious Henry had discovered "that the civilization of their manners and the reform of their clergy were benefits which the Irish ought cheerfully to purchase with the loss of their independence". [Lingard, *History of England* (abridged edition), 1867, p. 132].

Among the Norman barons who formed the spearhead of the invasion were adventurers from the Welsh Marches, in blood partly Nordic and French and partly Welsh. They included Richard de Clare, the earl of Pembroke, commonly called Strongbow, whose tomb still stands in Christ Church Cathedral, Dublin; Robert Fitz Stephen and Raymond le Gros; Milo de Cogan and Maurice Fitz Gerald; de Courcy and de Burgo. Of these *conquistadores* it is Maurice Fitz Gerald whose descendants we must now study as he it was who was the progenitor of the Leinster and Munster Geraldines who developed into powerful families governing territories which ranked among the finest in the Europe of their day. The Leinster branch of the Geraldines eventually obtained estates in and around what is now county Kildare and became the earls of Kildare and dukes of Leinster. Their splendid eighteenth century mansion at Carton, near Maynooth, and Leinster House, at present the seat of the Oireachtas in Dublin, stand graciously as testimony in stone to the long-lived power of the Leinster Geraldines.

In the south the leaders of the Geraldines became the earls of Desmond, governing a territory which included the richest plains in Munster. This family continued in the direct line down to the year 1583 when the last effectual earl of Desmond was killed at Glenagenty [*Gleann-an-Ghinntigh*] about five miles to the east of Tralee, the spot where the earl was killed being called Bóthar-an-Iarla. With his tragic death the great house of Desmond came to an end. He left a son, James, called the *Parliamentary* earl of Desmond, and a nephew James Fitz Thomas, called the *Sugan* earl, but Garret the 16th of his line may, in effect, be called the last of a great race which perished in the war of annihilation which Elizabeth and her lieutenants waged in Munster.

The Irish pedigree of the family starts with Maurice, then Gerald (the first baron of Offaly), and then Maurice again. It was the first Maurice who came to Ireland with Strongbow, and who died in 1177. The next Maurice Fitz Gerald became the second Lord Offaly and was appointed Lord Justice of Ireland in 1229, again in 1232, and was buried at Youghal in the friary of the Franciscans or Friars Minor which he had founded in the southern end of that town. He left three sons the first of whom was Gerald Fitz Gerald, knight and third lord Offaly who died in 1286. He was the ancestor of the earls of Kildare and dukes of Leinster through his grandson John Fitz Thomas Fitz Gerald who was created Earl of Kildare by letters patent dated the 14th May 1316 (9th Edward II).

Maurice's second son was Thomas Mor who, by his marriage with the daughter of Sir William Morris, obtained estates in Kerry and, having died at Youghal on the 26th May 1260, was buried in the Franciscan convent there, the completion of which building he had executed at his own expense. Thomas left one son Sir John Fitz Gerald, knight, who was the ancestor of the earls of Desmond. He was known as John of Callan because of his death, together with that of his son Maurice, at the battle of Callan in the present parish of Kilgarvan, barony of Glenarought [*Gleann Ua Ruachtain*] near Kenmare in the County of Kerry, in the year 1261, while at war with the Mac Carthy clan. It is stated in a manuscript that John was killed by Fineene Mac Carthy Reagh the year after his father's death and that both he and his son Maurice were buried in the Dominican priory at Tralee.

Sir John of Callan was married to Marjorie, a daughter of Sir Thomas Fitz Anthony, who was Seneschal of Leinster, and, by this marriage, he obtained large estates and became the first lord of Decies and Desmond. Their only son was Maurice who, as already stated, was killed together with his father in 1261. John Fitz Gerald of Callan founded the Dominican priory for the order of Preachers at Tralee about 1243 and built a strong castle there for his residence. His increasing power and conquests very naturally led to the hostility of the older Gaelic septs of Desmond (South Munster) who had to retreat to the south and west of Cork and Kerry before the advancing Normans who had occupied the great fertile plains and river valleys of Limerick, Cork and North Kerry.

Maurice, however, left a son Thomas who was called *na-nAppagh* or Thomas of the Ape. He received this name from the legend that a pet monkey of the family carried the child to the top of the family castle in Tralee when the household was thrown into disorder after the disaster at Callan. After some time it brought the child down and deposited it safely in the cradle. From that time the monkey has held an honourable place in the armorial bearings of the family.

This Thomas became very powerful in Munster. He was

baron of Offaly and was made Captain-General of Desmond and Lord Justice of Ireland in 1295 and, dying in 1298, left two sons. The elder was Maurice and, under the feudal law of primogeniture which the Normans brought to Ireland, he inherited the estates of his father not already granted *in vivos* or devised by will. Furthermore, on the 27th August 1329 (3rd Edward III) he was created the first Earl of Desmond and so began the title of that lordly branch of the Geraldines who, for two and a half centuries were the overlords of Munster and who had, as their chief stronghold, the ancient, walled and fortified town of Kilmallock in the centre of their vast domain.

It is now time to turn back the pages and return to Sir John of Callan and to the delicate, and often complicated, study of the fate of his four other children. These were Gilbert (or, in the Irish form, Gibbon), John, Maurice and Thomas. It is stated by many historians that John of Callan was married a second time and then to Honora, daughter of Hugh O'Connor-Kerry who was the sovereign lord and prince of the territory now known as the barony of Iraghticonnor in North Kerry adjoining which is the barony of Clanmaurice, and that these were her children by Sir John. Support for that statement is found in the well-known Russell and Cotter manuscripts relating to this family and in the pedigree written by the Chevalier O'Gorman on the FitzGibbon family for John FitzGibbon, Lord Chancellor of Ireland and the 1st earl of Clare. In his *Antiquarian Researches*, under the heading "Geraldine Knights", Sir William Betham says at volume I, page 229: "It has been asserted that these Knights were descended from illegitimate children of the Earl of Desmond; and it is found so stated in pedigrees . . . of Sir George Carew, afterwards Lord Totness, Lord President of Munster and Lord Deputy of Ireland, in the reign of Elizabeth. But this statement must be erroneous, for I find the Knight of Glynn mentioned on the records before the date of the creation of the earldom of Desmond, in 1329." He adds at page 234: "It has generally been supposed that these were titles granted by the Earls of Desmond as palatine earls of the County of Kerry; but this is not possible, for two of them, the White Knight and the Knight of Glynn, are not within his palatine jurisdiction; besides, they existed in the reign of Henry the Third, one hundred years before the creation of the earldom of Desmond, in 1329, in the great uncles of the first Earl of Desmond."

Also, according to several old Irish manuscripts, corroborated by ancient records such as the patent plea and pipe rolls, the descent of these sons is given as follows:—

John Fitz Thomas Fitz Gerald, first Lord of Decies and Desmond, married a second wife, Honora, daughter of O'Connor-Kerry, by whom he had four sons:

1. Gilbert (or, in the Irish, Gibbon) from whom is descended the White Knight.

2. John, ancestor of the Knight of Glin or the Valley.

3. Maurice, from whom the Knight of Kerry descended, and

4. Thomas, ancestor to the Fitz Geralds 'of the island of Kerry' or Castleisland, (*Oilean Chiarraighe*) in Trughanacmy (*Triucha-an-aicme*: the cantred of the sept) and Corcaguiny (*Corca Duibhne*). Some historians, however, say that Thomas left no issue and that this branch of the Fitz Geralds are the issue of a collateral branch of the family. The word 'cantred' used in the phrase 'cantred of the sept' (*supra*) was a hundred manors or villages and is represented in England by the phrase 'an hundred'.

These four children received from their step-nephew, Thomas-na-nAppagh (the father of the first Earl of Desmond), grants of land in Limerick and Kerry and in the conveyance the grantor uses the phrase "my father's brother" which is a strong presumption of legitimacy. Many Irish annalists, contrary to the testimony of the manuscripts and of Sir George Carew, held that there was

103

no such second marriage and that these four children of Sir John were illegitimate. But the Gaelic Irish had lost much of their lands to the Normans and it is natural to expect them to be biased. However, a pedigree of the earls of Desmond preserved in the British Museum states that John of Callan had married twice and that the second wife (the mother of these four children) was Honora "daughter of Phelim Mac Hugh O'Connor [of Cannaught]". The balance of probabilities would appear to be in favour of John of Callan having allied himself with O'Connor [Kerry] as being more likely to strengthen the local influence of the Geraldines.

As John of Callan was at war with the Clancarty (the Mac Carthys) at the time, it is stated repeatedly in various manuscripts that he sent these four children to foster-parents for their safety and education. Gibbon was fostered by O'Cunneen, John by O'Cuilleain, Maurice by O'Kennedy and Thomas by O'Connor and they are referred to often by the names of their foster-parents. Some of the Irish annalists argue from this assumption of the foster-name that they were illegitimate but, in ancient Irish society, fosterage, much like our modern adoption, created a spiritual relationship closely assimilated to that of blood relationship and almost indistinguishable from the relationship of true father and true son. The four children remained with the foster-parents until the Fitz Geralds regained their power.

As a result of such fosterage and of such inter-marriage these and other Anglo-Norman knights soon became intermingled with Irish families and they became neither more nor less than Irish chieftains with Norman names:

> Those Geraldines, those Geraldines, not long our air
> they breathed,
> Not long they fed on venison, in Irish water seethed;
> Not often had their children been by Irish mothers
> nursed,
> When, from their full and genial hearts, an Irish
> feeling burst.

The English monarch strove in vain, by law, and force,
  and bribe,
To win, from Irish thoughts and ways, this *more* than
  Irish tribe;
For still they clung to fosterage, to brehon, cloak, and
  bard;
What king dare say to Geraldine, your Irish wife
  discard?

Thomas-na-nAppagh, to whom the estates of John of
Callan and of his son Maurice passed under the Norman
law of primogeniture, made grants of land to each of his
four step-uncles. Gibbon, the son who was ancestor to the
White Knights, received the lands of Meane or
Mahownagh which were situate in the barony of Connello
in West Limerick and which names are almost
synonymous with the Irish word meadhon meaning
middle. In the reign of Mary Tudor, however, the White
Knight of that period and his kinsmen released to James,
the earl of Desmond, all their lands in Connello, viz. the
manors of Meane and Ballytine and the short castle at
Askeaton etc. They, however, retained their lands in
South-East Limerick and in North Cork in the barony of
Condons and Clangibbon. Sir William Betham says: "To
Gibbon the eldest of these sons [his father] gave the
manors of Castletown and Mitchelstown in the County of
Cork and other large possessions." Gibbon had inherited a
large tract of land in Limerick and Cork stated to be twenty
four miles in length and twelve miles in breadth which was
confirmed to him by letters patent of King Henry III in
1270. Gibbon's son Maurice was called Mac Gibbon, i.e. the
son of Gibbon, as were his descendants. By the Irish they
were also called Clan Gibbon, i.e. the tribe or family of
Gibbon. By the Hiberno-Normans they were later called
Fitz-Gibbon.

Maurice received lands in Kerry and was the ancestor
of the Knights of Kerry whose kinsmen still sometimes
reside near Ardfert, the ancient ecclesiastical capital of the
Norman lands of the north Kerry plains. John received

lands on the Shannon with the Castle of Glyn and Castletown. The descendants of John, the Knights of Glin and Lords of Clenglish, continued their race in the direct line and the present family home is in a Georgan mansion on the Shannon near the town of Glin, some distance from which is the ancient Glyn Castle. The last occupier of the lands of Clenglish was Sir John FitzGerald who fought with King James II and went to France after 1691 with the Irish Brigade. The youngest of John of Callan's sons was Thomas. Some historians say he was the progenitor of various families of the FitzGeralds in County Limerick and at Castleisland in the barony of Trughanacmy and at Corcaguiny in Kerry. The question of his having issue is, however, not clearly answered. In the former barony are the Gleanna Ruddery mountains and the Knight's mountain, associated with this family.

In these early days all persons who held land on tenure by knight-service were compellable to take knighthood under penalty of a fine. In fact all persons of high rank took the honour and a nobleman who was not a knight was always styled esquire.

As to how the knighthoods were obtained by these kinsmen and became hereditary is a matter of some controversy (see Sir William Betham, supra). The nature of hereditary knightly titles borne by the several branches of the Desmond Geraldines cannot be explained simply by the usages of the feudal system. That the honour of knighthood should be inherited would be contrary to all principles of chivalry. It is a strictly personal honour only to be won by deeds of valour and daring in the field. The hereditary transmisson of the knightly title was never legalised until James I invented the grade of Baronet largely to finance the plantation of Ulster. The possible explanation of this anomaly seems to be that these titles were transmitted by Irish usage and, in this respect, it must be remembered that the Geraldines of Desmond were among those who became "more Irish than the Irish themselves" by adapting many of the customs and assuming the distinctive rights of Irish chieftains. When the heads of certain Geraldine families had once been knighted, either by the king, the viceroy, or by their own seigneur, the Earl of Desmond, the title came to be transmitted by the Irish custom and even the earldom itself was frequently conferred on the most stalworth member of the race, setting aside the direct male heir.

One account of the origin of the knighthoods concerning these Geraldine brothers relates to the attendance of three of their sons with the armies of King Edward III in Scotland at the battle of Halidon Hill, fought near Edinburgh on July 19th 1333. It is a matter of history that a large Irish force attended Edward III in Scotland at this period. Writs of summons were sent to the earls of Ormonde and Desmond, to 55 knights, 14 princes and chiefs, and to 111 esquires, commanding them to attend with horses and arms the Lord Justice Darcy into Scotland "against the king's enemies and rebels". The Lord Justice Darcy with a large force passed from Ulster into Scotland and contributed effectively to the victory gained at Halidon Hill. In a manuscript, apparently written after the restoration of Charles II, which purports to give the pedigrees of the White Knight together with some passages relating to the Knight of Glin or the Valley (called the Black Knight), the Knight of Kerry (called the Green Knight), and the younger brother who, the manuscript states, (probably incorrectly) was the Lord of Clenglish, it is stated: "Now let the reader knowe that when the three Knights were first knighted they were not then brothers but all three were the sons of these three brothers . . . for we find that the name of the first White Knight was Sir Maurice and not Sir Gilbert or Sir Gibbon and that it was Maurice Fitz Thomas son of Thomas (A n'Appaig) the heyre afore often mentioned was Earl of Desmond when they were Knighted beng the first Earl of Desmond in whose days being in Anno 1326."

The same chronicler goes on to give a vivid description of the battle of Halidon Hill, the prowess of the three cousins to whom their kinsman, the earl of Desmond, had given each 2000 men to command, and the gallantry of

107

Maurice towards the ladies of the Scottish Royal Palace when the Scots were defeated and who was "of noe lesse generossitye and meekenesse among Ladyes than of courage and prowess among his enimys". He then goes on to state that the three cousins were presented to the king, armed as they had fought in battle each of them being somewhat wounded and the blood yet flowing. Maurice was stated to be deeply wounded in the left arm, under the shoulder "which the king perceiving, with his owne hands bound up with a white scarfe and black ribbond; and hense it came that the White Knights eaver since bear a white and black crosse in theyre field colours. In this manner the king presently knighted him in that field, and called him Maurice the White Knight as a distinction from the other two by reason that he wore a bright glittering armour. He then also knighted the other two, nameing them likewise after the colours of theyre armours in which they fought; for the second wearing Black armour was called the Black Knight; and the other who wore a greenish azure armour, was called the Greene Knight."

Accordingly, however apocryphal may be this account of what happened in Scotland in connection with Maurice the first White Knight, it is probable that he was there in the retinue of his feudal lord about this period, although it is impossible to say whether he was at the fight at Halidon Hill or not. Some historians say that Maurice was called the White Knight because he was fair-haired and indeed this explanation would appear to be in accordance with the Irish custom (although lacking the romance of the Halidon Hill story) by which people were often known by the colour of their hair. The names of Owen Roe and Hugh Dubh O'Neill, Red Hugh O'Donnell and Donnach Ruadh Mac Conmara are well-known examples of this common Irish usage. The earliest unambigious evidence, however, which is available as to these three hereditary knightly titles relates to a written pardon granted and attested by Henry VII on the 26th August, 1496, to the earl of Desmond and others including Domino Mauricio, le White Knight: Domino Mauricio Militi de Kerrye and Domino Edmundo

Militi de Waley. These pardons appear to have been granted for complicity in the rebellion of Perkin Warbeck.

We must now leave aside the story of the other knights and turn our full attention solely to the pedigree of Maurice, the first White Knight. How long he tarried in Scotland is uncertain but, while there, he married a Scottish lady named Katherine. He then went to England where he resided for some years and had issue by her two sons, Maurice and David, and two daughters, of which the elder married an English nobleman and the younger married Lord Barrymore . The White Knight having eventually returned to Ireland with his wife, who died shortly afterwards, gave himself up to piety and devotion and took on the habit of St. Dominic in the friary of St. Saviour at Kilmallock. This monastery, the extensive ruins of which still survive, and which are always referred to locally as the "Abbey" of Kilmallock, was founded by some Dominican priests in 1291 and was probably built under the patronage of Gibbon, the eldest son of Sir John of Callan by his second marriage, and completed by his son Maurice who now entered its cloisters. In a de Burgo manuscript, the author of which is explicit as to the legitimacy of the four brothers, it is stated:—

> This monastery was built by the grand-uncle of the before-mentioned Earl of Desmond — that is Gilbert Geraldine in Irish Gibbon, being the second of the sons of John of Callan the founder of our convent at Tralee, ancestor of the White Knight, as they call him, or of the Clan Gibbon, and of the entire family to which the surname Fitz Gibbon is given.

Maurice also built Courtnaruddery (*Cuirt an Ridire*), or the Knight's Castle, outside the walls of the medieval town of Kilmallock and, although it has long ceased to exist, its site is believed to be on the right bank of the river Lubach a short distance upstream from the north bridge.

Maurice did not stay long in the "Abbey" of Kilmallock but moved to the monastery at Youghal where he died in

1357, being then about sixty years of age. He was, however, buried at Kilmallock beside his wife in a tomb which he had erected for her during his lifetime. This tomb-niche is of elaborate construction and the tracery, of pointed arch and rounded shaft, still testifies to the loving care once bestowed upon it. Here lie the remains of the first traditional White Knight and his Scottish lady, the "toilsome cares and affairs of the world" troubling him now no more.

The elder son of this first White Knight was named Maurice like his father. Under the law of primogeniture the estates would pass to him and he would, apparently, become also the second White Knight but Maurice "went on a pilgrimage" leaving his younger brother David to succeed to the property and the knighthood. Maurice was called "Sean Riddery" or the "Old Knight" and, having married a daughter of lord Bourke, his issue was referred to as "Mac an tShan Riddery" or the "descendant of the old knight". Through this line descent has been traced to Maurice FitzGibbon of Chrohana House in the County of Kilkenny, in the last century, and it was argued that he then represented the family of the White Knights on the collateral side, the line of the traditional knighthood having become extinct in the 17th century.

David, the second White Knight, is stated to have married a daughter of the earl of Worcester but this is erroneous as the only Earl of Worcester with whose offspring David could have matched died without issue. At this period, however, there were Worcesters in Ireland with whom a marriage alliance would have strengthened his local influence. Philip of Worcester, Governor of Ireland in 1184-5, had a grant in 1215 of five cantreds in South Tipperary, including Knockgraffon, Ardfinan and several parcels of land lying close to what was afterwards to become known as the "White Knight's Country". The probability of this marriage is strengthened by the fact that a later White Knight, John Og Fitz Gibbon, who was attainted for high treason was, at that time, seized of portion of the manor of Knockgraffon, the ancient property of the de Wygornias (Worcesters) in Ireland and which subsequently came into possession of Sir William Fenton through his wife Margaret, the grand-daughter of Edmund Fitz Gibbon, the son of John Og.

David's heir was John who married Isabella, a daughter of the Lord Butler. He became the third White Knight and had issue Maurice as son and heir to the lands and knighthood. It is stated by the chronicler of the reign of Charles II (*supra*), that Maurice was knighted *de novo* in the field of battle for his services with his overlord, the earl of Desmond, during the insurrection of the Welsh under Owen Glendower in 1402 and that King Henry IV confirmed Maurice in the lands of his ancestors in Ireland — "and alsoe libertye to adde thereunto what hee could". But these events are not mentioned in the Irish or English chronicles of the period nor recorded in the English or Irish Rolls of Chancery.

Maurice, the fourth White Knight, married the daughter of Cormac Mac Carthy by whom he is stated to have had eight sons, of whom the heir was John who succeeded to the inheritance. Some of the sons obtained property in the townlands of Ardskeagh and Garryancoonagh, in Cork and Limerick respectively, while other lands stretched from the townland of Knocklary on the Morningstar river to Athadiberty, "the ford of the small Dibert stream" near Kilmallock, and from thence southwards to the top of Sliever Reagh, or the brown mountain, which rises to the east of Kilfinane.

John, the fifth White Knight, married Margaret the daughter of O'Brien by whom he had issue Maurice and William the Blind. William built the castle of Old Castletown on a rock, formerly called Magner's Rock, near Kildorrery, County Cork, and which later became an important property of the White Knights. Maurice succeeded his father the as sixth White Knight, and married the daughter of O'Sullivan Beare by whom he had issue John. He also married a second wife, the widow of Thomas, the eighth earl of Desmond, who had been beheaded at Drogheda in 1467. Of this marriage there was also issue. On the death of Maurice, the countess, his widow, based

111

the claim of *her* eldest son by him to the title and estates of the White Knight "upon pretence that pursuant to a marriage settlement with Maurice her late husband", the White Knight's estate was to devolve upon Gibbon her son and not upon John. Gibbon entered into possession of the inheritance as the seventh White Knight and, driven to desperation, John appealed to his half-brother, who was then living in the castle at Mitchelstown, for a livelihood in his native country. This Gibbon refused and, on pursuing him from the castle, Gibbon was caught by a few of John's loyal retainers and hanged. John proceeded to Youghal to the earl of Desmond and then sought the protection of the earl of Kildare to whom he poured out all his grievances and, as a result, he took peaceful possession of all his inheritance, becoming the eighth White Knight.

By his marriage John had issue two sons, John and Thomas, and one daughter. The second son, Thomas, was the ancestor of the FitzGibbons of Ballylanders in County Limerick from which parish the ancestors of John FitzGibbon, the 1st earl of Clare, originated. John succeeded his father as the ninth White Knight and, by his marriage to Joan, the daughter of Lord Barrymore, he had four sons, Maurice, John, Thomas and Gibbon. The eldest son, Maurice, died in the lifetime of his father leaving a son, also called John, who eventually succeeded to the title and estates but who proved harsh towards his uncles on the death of their father. Strife resulted and the tenth White Knight was slain by his uncles, whereupon the earl of Desmond summoned David FitzGibbon of Ballylanders to meet him on the hill of Kilmallock, together with his followers, so that he might confirm him in the inheritance and there to call him White Knight. Having assembled on the hill, however, David declined the honour and eventually John Og, the uncle who had procured the death of his nephew, the tenth White Knight, succeeded as eleventh White Knight, after his reconciliation with the house of Desmond. He was a man of very turbulent spirit and, after the reconciliation, he allied himself with the earl in the confederacy against Elizabeth. During the religious persecutions he gave sanctuary to many of the clergy, particularly the Dominicans, to whose protection many came from all parts of the kingdom. In the aforesaid ms., of the reign of Charles II it is stated that he was hardly ever free from crosses and troubles "which, notwithstanding, he valued not but bore them out stoutly as it were one man against the whole world . . . and was a man unequalled in his dayes for bodyly strength and courage of minde". He died at Kilmallock in 1569 and was buried in the Dominican friary there. Two years after his death he was attainted for high treason and all his estate escheated to the Crown excepting the rights of his widow either by inheritance or dower.

John Og had married Ellen, the daughter of Patrick Condon of the barony of Condons and Clangibbon. The Condons were generally in close alliance with their neighbours the White Knights (after whom the barony was jointly named), although both families sometimes harried each other's lands. Their common enemy were the Roches of Fermoy and the Condons eventually lost all their fine estate of about 6,000 acres in the Confederate Wars of 1641.

Maurice, the eldest son of John Og, was killed in 1568 at Clogher, near Lixnaw, in Kerry, together with seventeen other heirs of noblemen, in a dispute between Garret, earl of Desmond, and Fitzmaurice of Kerry and, on the death of his father, Edmund, the second son, became the twelfth White Knight but was reduced to poverty by the forfeiture of his father's possessions. The Crown, however, in 1576 gave Edmund a lease of a large portion of the forfeited lands in the adjoining areas of Limerick, Tipperary and Cork for twenty-one years. In 1579, Edmund surrendered this lease and received a fresh grant comprising a larger area and, in 1590, these leases were converted into a grant in tail male at a certain rent "in consideration of the faithful painful and dangerous services done unto us by Edmond Fitz Gibbon, usually called the White Knight, and in consideration also that his father's lands to which he was inheritable were by some hard construction of law, though justly, seized for us and by us granted to his son now called Edmond Gybbon in lease for years."

In the following year he obtained a further grant of some of his father's possessions, including "chief rents out of Kilfynan [Kilfinane] in the tenure of Shane boye Roche" and "the site of the castle of Court Rudderye near the town of Kilmallock . . . to hold in tail male *in capite*". It is probable, however, that the favour just shown to Edmund was at the expense of other members of the family especially the "Old Knight's" sept and, by a Chancery inquisition taken at Kilmallock in 1608, it was found that Maurice, the son of Edmund, was seized of Ballinlandry (Ballylanders) and Callan but that kinsmen of Maurice had claimed the lands by inheritance. Continued disputes, in fact, existed regarding the lands granted to Edmund by the Crown whose right to grant them was questioned by the parties who were in possession at the time of the attainder of John Og Fitz Gibbon.

Edmund went to the continent with James Fitz Maurice Fitz Gerald in 1575 but later he performed "memorable acts for the Crowne of England . . . for which services hee obtayned a good part of his father's estate and would have undoubtedly have gotten it all, but his death and other crosses in his life prevented it." In the aforesaid ms. the writer states that it was hereditary for him to have valour and boldness of courage, and, as to the charge that he was cruel and fierce in time of war, "he was severe to such as he found disloyall to ye Crowne of England", but that "such was his fervick heart and valorous spirit that the greatest and stoutest of the land in his dayes was not able to compare with him." However, Edmund's loyalty to the Crown was often suspect and he was accused of sundry treasons after the proclamation of the earl of Desmond as traitor. The accusations were made to Ormonde by the Roches — not a very reliable source in the circumstances! — but Sir Nicholas Malby, writing to the Earl of Leicester in 1582, said that the earl of Desmond was very strong; that Fitz Maurice of Kerry had joined with him, that it was

114

rumoured that the White Knight had revolted and that his son was in Spain in search of foreign aid. The White Knight was, in fact, kept under strict supervision if not actual confinement for a period in Dublin Castle by Perrott who proposed to send him, Patrick Condon, and others to England while large areas of the lands of his father, John Og Fitz Gibbon, went to strangers who received "parcels here and there of the White Knight's country". Many of Elizabeth's officials in Munster of course wished for a share of the rich territories which would fall to the Crown by the destruction of the house of Desmond and the Fitz Gibbons. Among the most active of these was the astute Sir Warham St. Leger, ancestor of the Doneraile family.

From the time of his father's death in 1569 the life of Edmund, as of most of the great Anglo-Irish lords of Munster, had been spent in armed resistance to the order of things proposed by the queen's officers in that province. This system of government contemplated the abolition of all chieftainship whether English or Irish, the extinction of all usages of tanistry and the dissipation of the great Irish properties. From the first outbreak of James Fitz Maurice Fitz Gerald in 1577, until the period immediately preceding the battle of Kinsale in 1601, this struggle continued unbroken and in all the troubles up to the final catastrophe the White Knight had taken a part.

The conduct of the White Knight with regard to the proceedings of the earl of Tyrone and his invasion of Munster was characterised by something more than inconsistency. Closely watched as he was by the lord president and his active spies, Edmund Fitz Gibbon was on his guard, but there can be little doubt that he faithfully promised to join the earl and afterwards held aloof from all complicity in a movement which ended so disastrously at Kinsale. The strength of the White Knight at this time was considerable and he was included by the English among the most powerful of the Munster chieftains. In a letter written by Carew to Sir Robert Cecil in 1600 he states that Fitz Gibbon had sent many messages to him promising allegiance but he was suspicious of this promise

115

of fealty, for "a more faythlesse man never lived upon the earthe", and the one thing which could win Edmund over to the queen was "the internall malice betwene James Mac Thomas [the *Sugan* earl of Desmond] and him which is irreconcilable." On the 22nd of May, 1600 the White Knight made his humble submission to the lord president near Kilmallock and then attended him as far as Limerick. Cecil did not place much faith in Edmund's professions of loyalty but Carew looked upon the event with much satisfaction, laying the credit for it with his subordinate, Sir George Thornton, for "the White Knight is the most wyse, subtill and valliant man in Mounster and of great following".

Eventually, on the 29th May, 1601, the *Sugan* earl was captured by the White Knight and some followers in a cave traditionally believed to be the one which is since known as "The Desmond Cave" (but previously called "Oonacara-greisha" — The cave of the Grey Sheep) in the townland of Coolagarranroe, Co. Tipperary. The cave consists of numerous natural vaulted passages extending into the mountain limestone formation of which the entire district is formed, and is one of the two adjoining but unconnected caves well-known as The Mitchelstown Caves. The captured earl was brought to Kilbehenny Castle and eventually handed over to the lord president at Shandon Castle, Cork.

Edmund had married Joan Tobyn, daughter of the lord of Cumshionagh of County Tipperary, by whom he had issue two sons, Maurice and John, and four daughters. Maurice, the heir, married Joan Butler, the daughter of the lord of Dunboyne, by whom he had issue Maurice Og and Margaret. Maurice the son of Edmund died at Old Castletown on the 22nd of April, 1608, the day before his father's death at Kilbehenny. He was buried with his father in the church at Kilbehenny and, after a week, the remains of both were removed to Kilmallock where they still lie under a slab which marks the grave in the floor of the chancel of the Dominican friary. John, the second son, died at Bristol, where he was sent to take a cure at the

Bath, and was buried near that city. The death of Edmund was for all practical purposes the end of the White Knights as Maurice Og, his grandson who succeeded as the thirteenth White Knight, died without issue on the 20th of May, 1611, about the age of fourteen years, soon after his marriage to Thomasin, daughter of Sir Thomas Browne of Hospital, Co. Limerick. Since the death of Maurice Og the title of White Knight has remained in abeyance although claims to the title have been made by descendants on the female side. Soon after the death of Edmund a determined attempt was made to obtain the extensive estates by adventurers but the lands were, in fact, granted in 1618 to Sir William Fenton and his wife, Dame Margaret Fenton, who was the granddaughter of Edmund Fitz Gibbon the last effectual member of the family of White Knights.

APPENDIX

Pedigree of the White Knights

MAURICE FITZGERALD — Came to Ireland with Strongbow in 1169 — died 1177

|

GERALD — The first Lord Offaly

|

MAURICE — The second Lord Offaly

|

THOMAS MOR — Died 1260

|

JOHN — The first Lord of Decies and Desmond — killed at the Battle of Callan, near Kenmare, Co. Kerry, in 1261.

|

GILBERT or GIBBON — Eldest son of John's second marriage — the progenitor of the FitzGibbons.

|

MAURICE — The first White Knight — knighted after the Battle of Halidon Hill, near Edinburgh, Scotland, in 1333 — died 1357 at Youghal and buried at Kilmallock.

|

DAVID — The second White Knight.

|

JOHN — The third White Knight.

|

MAURICE — The fourth White Knight — knighted *de novo* at Chepstow by the King of England in 1402 — died 1419.

JOHN — The fifth White Knight.

|

MAURICE — The sixth White Knight.

|

GIBBON — The seventh White Knight — a son of
Maurice's second marriage, he usurped the title.

|

JOHN — The eight White Knight.

|

JOHN — The ninth White Knight.

|

MAURICE

|

JOHN — The tenth White Knight.

|

JOHN OGE — The eleventh White Knight — died 1569
— posthumously attainted for high treason and
deprived of his lands.

|

EDMUND — The twelfth and last *effectual* White
Knight — recovered most of his father's lands — died
1608.

|

MAURICE — Died in 1608, one day before his father's
death.

|

MAURICE OGE — The thirteenth and last White
Knight — died at the age of fourteen, in 1611.

SELECT BIBLIOGRAPHY

J.G. Barry, "Limerick during the Reign of Queen Elizabeth", JLFC, I:I (1897), 1-19.

J. Begley, *The Diocese of Limerick in the Sixteenth and Seventeenth Centuries*, Dublin 1927.

J.C. Coleman, *The Caves of Ireland, Tralee 1965.*

B. FitzGerald, *The Geraldines*, London 1951.

D.J. Gargan, *The Desmond Cave of Mitchelstown*, Dublin 1939.

Capt. Gerrard, "Gerrards and Geraldines", JCHAS, 34 (1929), 30-35 and 71-75.

J.Graves (editor), "Unpublished Geraldine Documents, Part II: The Pedigree of the Geraldines of Desmond", JRSAI, 10 (1868-69), 459-559.

J. Graves (editor) "Unpublished Geraldine Documents, Part IV: The Whyte Knight", JRSAI, II(1870-71), 591-640 and 15 (1879- 82), 640-730.

S. Hayman (editor), "Unpublished Geraldine Documents, Part 1: Russell's 'Relation of the FitzGeralds of Ireland'" JRSAI, 10 (1868-69), 356-416.

G.G. Hewson, "Notes on the Pedigree of The White Knight", JRSAI, 16 (1883-84), 65-67.

G.A. Lee, "Medieval Kilmallock", NMAJ, 9 (1962-65), 145-154.

A complete series of documents, known as the "Unpublished Geraldine Documents" were edited from about the year 1868 down to 1882 by the Rev. Canon Hayman, the Rev. James Graves, Miss Agnes Hickson and Mr. W.M. Hennessy and published, at intervals, in the Journal of the Royal Society of Antiquaries of Ireland. The intervals between publication were occupied by the editors "in an exhaustive search in every conceivable source, whence reliable information concerning the subject in hand was likely to be obtained". The present essay is a summary, in a simplified form, from the rich harvest of information which the editors collected over the years and the writer is indebted almost entirely to the labours of those who collected and edited these documents for the contents of this essay.

Robert Dwyer Joyce

A POET OF THE LEGENDS OF IRELAND

It was at Glenosheen in the heart of the Ballyhoura mountains, which extend eastwards from Charleville to the Galtee foothills, that Robert Dwyer Joyce was born and there he spent his early life. Here in this lovely border country with its wooded hills, its numerous mountain streams and lonely glens, overlooking the great Limerick plain, is an environment worthy of a poet; and here, too, is a land rich in legend and historic record, of which the author has made full use in his charming *Ballads of Irish Chivalry*, first published in 1861 under the title *Ballads, Romances and Songs* when he was a medical student in Cork.

The second edition, which contained many new poems, was published in 1872 when the author was a physician in practice at Boston but, soon after coming from the press, it was destroyed in the great Boston fire of that year. In 1908 his brother, P.W. Joyce, the poet and historian edited a selection of the ballads which, with the exception of a few well-known pieces, came before the people with all the freshness of a new publication.

In the ballads we have preserved many of the legends which were common in the Irish countryside a century ago but which are either fast disappearing or have already been forgotten by the descendants of those who told them around the fireside in the less sophisticated days of the poet's youth. Here we find revealed not merely the author's knowledge of the legends of the south, and his love for Ireland, as shown in his ballads on Sarsfield's ride to Ballyneety and the defence of Limerick but also his deep love for the countryside and, in particular, for his own homeland in the heart of Ballyhoura.

Thus in *The Well of Omen* he tells the legend of the shadows which was current around Ardpatrick, a green hill two miles west of Kilfinane with its abbey ruin and churchyard, in the early part of the last century:

> *There is a well sunk deeply by old Ard-Patrick's wall;*
> *Within it gaze the peasants to see what may befall:*
> *Who see their shadows down below, they will have*
>   *merry cheer;*
> *Who see not any shadows shall die within the year."*

This well was originally contructed more than a thousand years ago to provide the community of monks with water long before the enclosure was turned into a graveyard.

In his *Song of the Forest Fairy* the author strikes a happier note:

> *Where the gold moss hangs on the mighty oak,*
> *Where never was heard the woodman's stroke,*
> *In the ancient woods*
> *Where the wild deer bide—*
> *Where the heron broods*
> *By the lakelet's side,*
> *Morn, noon and eve, in the rosy air,*
> *We dance and sport full merrily there.*
>
> *'Tis glorious to see the globes of dew*
> *By the red beams of morn pierced through and*
>   *through;*
> *'Tis sweet to peer*
> *Where the wild flower gleams,*
> *And sweeter to hear*
> *The birds and the streams;*
> *And sweeter than all in the blue, bright air,*
> *To dance and sport so merrily there.*

A legendary figure that is commemorated not only in

123

song and story but also in place-names all over Ireland, as well as in the highlands of Scotland, is that of the Gadaighe Dubh O Dubháin. Robert Dwyer Joyce relates an incident in the life of the Black Robber, the scene of the story being laid in Glenagaddy (the glen of the robber) in Blackrock mountain between Ardpatrick and Glenosheen. Here he describes the home of the Black Robber near "a waterfall brown and clear" which forms a little stream called the Noneen and gives the name to Ballynahown (the town of the river). Before joining the Loobagh at Kilmallock the stream flows near the hamlet of Ballingaddy, again so named from the legend of the Black Robber.

Perhaps the poet is at his best when he describes the country-side around Glenanaar (the glen of slaughter). This wild valley, in the mountains between Doneraile and Kilfinane through which flows the Aunanaar, has been made famous by Canon Sheehan's book of that name in which is told in dramatic form the story of the so-called Doneraile conspiracy and the night ride from Cork across the mountains of Muskerry to Derrynane to brief O'Connell in defence of the accused men at the Cork assizes.

Describing this area, Joyce says:

Grand are the mountains that circle Glenara,
Seefin and brown Corrin, Knockea, and Slieve Darra;
Proudly their summits look down where its sheen flood
Lies coiled in the gorges or sunk in the greenwood.

Sweet are the scenes where that clear flood enlarges,
Peaceful and homes by its flower-scented marges;
Fair are the maidens with eyes brightly glowing,
Who bide by its windings and list to its flowing.

Robert Dwyer Joyce is also the author of two long poems, *Deirdré*, and *Blanid*, published in Boston in 1876 and 1879, respectively. Both are epic poems of the Red Branch era. In *Deirdré* the story commences with a banquet in the house of Feilimid, the story-teller to the king of Eman.

During the festivity Deirdré, the daughter of Feilimid, is born and Caffa prophesies her future beauty and the destruction it will bring on Eman and on the king and nobility. The nobles, thereupon, demand the death of the infant but the king orders her to be cloistered until she grows old enough to become his wife. In time Naisi, son of Usna, falls in love with Deirdre and he and his brothers carry her away to Alba where the Scottish king also comes to love her. He tries to compass the death of Naisi and his brothers, who escape with Deirdre to one of the Hebridean islands. Thence they are decoyed by the king of Eman who gives surety for their safety. On their return to Ireland the sons of Usna are slain on the green of Eman—

> *To-night, to-night,*
> *O sons of Usna, bitter is your plight,*
> *For you are compassed round by treachery;*
> *And dreadful is the deed the morn shall see,*
> *Wherefrom accurst with everlasting shame*
> *All men in wrath shall hold bright Eman's name!*

The poem ends with the lamentations and death of Deirdre, as—

> *Lowly upon her husband's breast she laid*
> *Her bright head, and great moans of anguish made*
> *That soon grew still.*
> *And lay there never more to rise again,*
> *And live for love, and fight with grief and pain!*

The second poem is founded on the story of the tragic death of Curoi Mac Dáire from Caherconree. Blanid (The Blossom Bright), daughter of the king of Mana, who is sought in marriage by the princes of Western Europe, refuses them all and falls in love with Cuhullin, the son of her father's most powerful enemy. The princes form a league to win her and, gathering their fleets, sail for Dun Dalgan where they elect Cuhullin leader of the expedition. They besiege and sack the stronghold of Mana. At the distribution of the spoils Blanid, by a stratagem, is won and taken away by Curoi, prince of South Munster. Cuhullin pursues Curoi and overtakes him at the foot of the mountain of Blama, where they fight for the possession of Blanid. Cuhullin is vanquished and Curoi leads Blanid away in triumph to the south.

The lovers meet again and, with the help of Blanid's foster-mother, make a plot to slay Curoi. This is done on the night of the feast of Samhain and Blanid is borne away to Eman by Cuhullin. Curoi's minstrel follows them and at the hunting feast of Rincan-Beara, where he had been playing, he dashed down his harp—

> *And clutched the Bright One,*
> *and ere lord or knight*
> *Could rush between them, o'er the cliff he sprang*
> *Clutching her closely still;*
> *Along the height*
> *His last weird shout of vengeance lessening rang,*
> *As far beneath amid the breaker's roar*
> *They disappeared and ne'er were looked on more!*

Before writing these epic poems the author had published in Boston two small prose volumes — *Legends of the Wars in Ireland* and *Irish Fireside Tales* while several other of his prose stories, all with Irish themes, were contributed to various magazines. He returned to Dublin in 1883 and died on the 24th October of that year.

In the introduction to the first edition of the *Ballads*, the author stated that his object was to do for Ireland that which she would not have lacked had her old language remained dominant and her customs, so favourable to bardic literature, inviolate, or modified by friendly hands alone.

Dr. Joyce has merited a place in the Irish memory for his pioneering work in the preservation of a part of the ancient culture in the days before the rebirth of the nation had commenced.

Italian Journey

Italy! fairest Italy the land of art
Which Heaven hath blest with more than human
*   heart;*
Once more from memory's fondest choice
I hear the songs of Petrarch and Dante's mystic voice.

As the train emerged from the tunnels of Mont Cenis, leaving behind the rugged grandeur of French Savoy and the forgotten frontier village of Modane, it was easy to realize that we had entered Piedmont. For there in that green land at the foot of the mountains were elements symbolic of the Italian scene — the little yellow villages clustering on hillsides and topped by the slender campaniles of parish churches, the endless terraces of vines and olive trees like tiers in a fantastic theatre, the thin line of mountain rivers now reduced to the pale trickle of autumn streams and, everywhere, the dark green mantle of the pines high up on the mountain sides and almost to the snow-line.

On entering Turin I had the first big surprise of my Italian journey for here was no bomb-shattered industrial town but a city of gracious beauty. The lovely Via Roma which stretches through the heart of the city — the slender line of which is broken here and there by fountains, squares and the greenest of green parks — must certainly rank among the cleanest and most attractive shopping streets in Europe and, to the weary traveller from an absurdly overcrowded train, it had something of the atmosphere of a paradise regained.

Some of the individual glories of Turin had been lost in the bombing of 1942 — the interiors of many churches and of the 17th and 18th century Baroque palazzi but when one sat awhile in the spacious 18th century S. Carlo Square with its great equestrian statue, its long line of Fiat cars, the open-air cafes and the orchestra playing the waltzes of Vienna, it was difficult to believe, in that warm September afternoon, that this *piazza* had, in great part, but recently arisen from the ashes of 1942. But such was the case and that work of expert restoration was going on, or had already been completed, not only in Turin but in all the bombed corners of the North Italian towns.

On leaving the mountains the landscape quickly changed for we were now approaching the great irrigated plain of Lombardy with its rich red soil, its droves of labouring oxen, the maze of corn crops and orchards and, perhaps above all, the far vistas with many a tall campanile standing like a sentinel against the clear outline of the distant horizon.

From such a countryside it was pleasant to enter the city of Brescia; Brescia of the winding cobbled streets and shuttered windows where every other building was a palace with its courtyards and fountains; Brescia of the lovely Piazza Vecchia with its vast town hall, its arcades and the curious clock with double numbering according to the old Italian style. And if I should choose one place from among the many in these northern provinces as representing the traditional Italian town I would, with some hesitation for the claims of Vicenza or Trento, give the laurels to this city at the foot of the southern Alps. Brescia did not entirely escape the ruins of war and some of its monumental buildings were damaged or destroyed. But here, as almost everywhere in these areas, the losses from bombing seemed almost irrelevant when viewed in the light of all that remains and against a background of the age-old Latin genius for restoration.

After leaving the area of valley and low hills with their vines and cypress trees the road from Brescia to Riva del Garda became one of the engineering master-pieces of modern Italy. For this is the great highway which Mussolini, at the height of his power, had carved out of well-nigh thirty miles of sheer mountain along the length of the lake. Through this road with its long tunnels, at times like high Gothic vaults broken here and there by the streets and squares of the lakeside towns, the fine Fiat buses of the Dolomite Society travel from the northern mountain country before fanning out towards the cities of Lombardy.

The great city of Verona, with its palaces and squares, lived up to its reputation of being one of the grandest centres in Italy. Dante fled here from Florence in 1316 and, in the 15th century, the town was the centre of a distinguished school of painters whose works survive in volume in the municipal galleries. Here is the vast, almost intact, Roman amphitheatre in the Piazza Vittorio Emanuele, still the scene of opera and drama; here the Piazza delle Erbe, one of the most picturesque squares in Italy, formerly the forum and now the fruit and vegetables market with its marble column bearing the Lion of St. Mark to indicate the former supremacy of the Venetian Republic. Nearby is the smaller Piazza dei Signori with its stone pavements, its imposing buildings and exquisite statue of Dante in a mood very reminiscent of Goldsmith in College Green. Surely that beautiful little square, with the nearby tombs of the Scaligeri, who, for upwards of a century were presidents of the Republic of Verona is one of the loveliest corners of all that lovely land of Italy.

As elsewhere Verona paid its share of the tolls of war and, while few of its great monuments were destroyed, several were damaged but, with some exceptions, little of note in the city has been lost. Among the exceptions should be mentioned the monumental Ponte della Pietra, the earliest of all surviving Roman bridges, and the world-famous Ponte Scaligero, built by Cangrande II in 1354. Together with all the other Veronese bridges they were demolished on the 25th April 1945.

One of the most pleasant features of post-war restoration has been the erection of fine new railway stations and those at Verona, Vicenza and Bologna, with their beautiful brick and red-stone finish, were, one hoped, but examples of what these new buildings would be like throughout the bomb-shattered rail centres of Italy. Along the route to the Brenner Pass, with its vital supply line from Germany, few of the old stations survived and at most places the rebuilding had been completed, until, at Ala, one found the new station, with its shuttered windows and white plaster finish, more like a tourist hotel on the shores of Lake Garda.

Like many of the other cities of the north Trento and Padua had their share of ruin but, apart from the destruction of the world-famous Eremitani church at Padua, which, however, has been regarded as the greatest individual disaster to Italian art during the war, nothing of value has been lost. This old Augustinian church of the thirteenth century containing frescoes by Andrea Mantegna and his contemporaries, which were among the most important examples of northern Italian art, was struck by a stick of bombs in March 1944 and, apart from two of the frescoes by Mantegna which had been removed to Venice for safety, all the remaining perished. The nearby Arena chapel with its wonderful frescoes by Giotto was, however, quite intact and elsewhere the damage was slight in this historic city of St. Anthony with its great Basilica of Il Santo dating from the thirteenth century, its *piazze* and the eternal arcades which flank the narrow streets of the inner city.

The remarkable city of Vicenza, enhanced by many Palladian palaces of the sixteenth century, had suffered most from bombing among these northern towns but, while the list of damaged buildings conveys a melancholy story, nevertheless the great majority of the individual glories of the city, including the famous Piazza dei Signori, have survived intact and its character is essentially unchanged. Here indeed, among the works of restoration, pride of place had been given to the rebuilding of the cathedral which was officially described as practically destroyed at the end of hostilities. This rather unusual church with its broad low nave and aisles converted into chapels had once again assumed its old appearance. The chapels had all been re-erected; the roof had been replaced

130

and, although the original frescoes by Bartolommeo Montagna had been lost, one could not help thinking, now that the work had almost been completed, that the Duomo of Vicenza had the appearance more of normal restoration than abnormal reconstruction after the ruins of war.

In the course of my wanderings I had often wondered by what experience I should remember Italy the longest. Was it by the grand outline of the Piazza S. Marco at Venice with its peerless Duomo and palace of the Doge? Was it by the pleasant evenings spent beneath the olive trees on the shore of the lake, or by the sight of an autumn sunset bching the pinnacles of the Brescian Alps? And, as the time came to say farewell, I knew that it was by none of these experiences but by the memory of the people themselves that I would remember this southern country. For to-day, with its newly found prosperity, one remembers Italy, as it must always have been, by the crowds of happy children playing in the sunny squares, by the endless chatter and laughter of their elders and by the many old-world courtesies and the spiritual and human values so evident throughout the land and which, for all of us, can only become of increasing importance in a world that is daily becoming increasingly small.

Autumn Leaves

TO THE WEST WIND

Blow! thou clarion-call to happiness,
Blow from a land where sun is loath to die;
Come in thy cool, clear, crystal-streams of joy,
What if they lips are moist from clouds' caress?

Thy sister from the east with jealous breast,
With biting breath, the orphan of the sky
Has passed her arid way with stinging sigh,
With Judas-kiss and cunning smile unblest.

Flow gently like the fragrance of a flower
That bares its heart on summer days;
With grace and freshness bless the hour
When lovers meet on trysting-ways.

Fall softly like the sweetness of a shower
Or the magic of a myth from Doric lays.

What ceaseless change doth Beauty make
In forest old or sylvan glade,
What endless forms may Beauty take
For those who linger 'neath her shade;
Midst cobbled streets in cities fair
Or in the purity of air on mountain slopes,
When winter bare has stripped the larch
And beech trees' lair and given each
A garland rare of glistening white.
What joy is there, what surge of joy,
To gaze and look and feast the eye
On scenes so clear in land and sky;
What sadness too that these must die!
O spirit! thou has made for me
A willing bond from start of day
'Till summer eve, and I must bear
The pain of every lover's lay
Who sings his songs at Beauty's feet.
I love thee still and always will.

CITY LIGHTS

The gleaming lights are silent, need they speak?
Their saga is the saga of the blest;
By common way or on patrician peak
They keep a vigil for the noonday's rest.

With nervous dance they flicker on the bay
With certain smile they brighten up a street;
On classic facade is their epic lay
In city lane their ballad, less discreet.

In summer when the sylvan leaves are gay,
They form a ballet with the playful breeze,
In autumn, as the colours fade away,
A mourning for the dying trees.

AGHADOE

With the breeze came a whisper of friendship
Remote from the wanderings of men;
On the lake was a shimmer of landscape
Where the sunlight reflected the glen.

In the air was a rustle of spring-time,
Yet so faint, it had scarcely begun
And the clouds, as they strayed on their journey,
Gave the mountains a kiss, one by one.

In the centre lay famed Innisfallen
With its beauty of woodland and stone,
Yet so silent! its glories are vanished
Or they linger in legend alone.

All around me were symbols more ancient,
A churchyard, its yew trees and tower
And the quietness and fragrance of morning
Showered its peace on that emerald bower.

ODE TO SPRING

A tower, a spire, a tiny dome
Glinting in the sun;
The trees are barren of their leaves
Yet stately, every one.

The bay is calm, the boats have gone
And clouds are forming fast;
On stubble-brown the cattle browse
To wait the winter's past.

But somewhere in the western sky
The daylight lingers long,
With streaks of red and spectral blue
It sings a welcome song.

Come swiftly Spring when soft winds blow
Over moorland and glen in the morning light,
When shadows quicken in the evening glow
And winter lies sleeping in his cave of night.

No laughter waits upon me now;
All is silent and unsung
Within the garden of my life;
After years of toil
To gain a modest laurel for my brow
I am alone amidst the bitter-sweet
of lilacs in a windswept May.
All is dark or twilight-gray
Within my heart; along the way
The strands of time are falling from my hands
And do not stay beneath a heavy tread of feet
On shifting clay. O come that day!
When once again the dawn for me will bring
A stream of joy unknown to emperor or king,
Not as an image on a desert shore
Which the weary straggler vainly seeks to win,
But Peace which flows from God's eternal kin.

EVENING

A milk-calm sea! no anger spoils its stillness,
A milk-calm sea where passions lie at rest;
Touched only now, by mist and evening's mantle,
A milk-calm sea caressed.

No glare of light or arrow thrusts of sunset
Cut furrows on its bosom, pure and deep;
No sound, save from the nearby woodlands,
Of birds that sing their lullaby of sleep.

In the night a honey-glow of golden
From harvest-moon that hovers near the hill
Scatters wide the fast-encroaching darkness;
A mystic world where God is reigning still.

DAYDREAMS

I long for thee, when happiness is mine
Amidst the wind-swept air,
To come and linger, just a little while
And share the beauty there.

To watch a falling-star, at night,
With wondrous speed pass by
Or tiny blossoms floating on a brook
At noon, to die.

I think of thee when fleeting shadows on a hill
The changing sun unfolds,
And silken meadows, bending with the breeze,
Recall the joys of old.

I sigh for thee as loneliness comes near
When, through the echoes' call,
I hear thy laughing voice
And see thee through a tear-drop's fall.

MUSINGS

Oft in the quietness of a noon
I wander far by waterfall and stream
Thinking of my love; As in a dream
Her voice is echoed by the water's tune.

Oft when the evening-star is born
I see her in the radiance of it's light
And, when it's form has vanished with the flight
Of day, darkness makes my hope forlorn.

Sometimes at dawn when Venus casts its ray
On dewy slopes where autumn's mantle falls
A distant vision of that star recalls
The lover's solace with a new-born day.

THE RESURRECTION

It is that or nothing from day to day,
The traveller's joy at sunset hour,
The lodestar on the pilgrim's way,
For wearied steps a quiet bower.

It is that or nothing through darkened paths,
The barque upon the watery way,
When thought is pain and tears flow fast
And the hope of youth has fled away.

It is that or nothing when daylight's past
And darkness falls on death's decay,
God's kindly hand that holds you fast
And leads you towards the starry way.

143

SUMMER

Shimmering wavelets rippling on the sea
By rock-infested shore;
Magic and beauty as western winds
Through ancient turrets roar
And sorrows are no more.

Rugged hilltops reaching for the sky
By cloudlets' faery bower;
Laughter and joy when children's voices
Through friendly breezes soar
And solitude is no more.

The wearied sun creeping to its lair
And evening's silent core;
Stillness and prayer while moonlight beams
Through twilight's mantle pour
And sadness is no more.

WET AND WINDSWEPT MAY

O cheerless sky for ever gray!
Are tears the only gifts you bring
To mortal man and sodden clay,
When life beneath you longs to sing
A joyous song, a laughing lay,
Upon the spring-time of its day?

Trees and grass and flowers of May
Are weeping too, their dirge in tune,
With wind and rain their only play
And early promise lost too soon;
While petals droop as though to pray
At sylvan shrines along their way.

HAIL AND FAREWELL

This too shall pass away
Like a snowdrop in the spring,
Birth and death and everything,
The harvest of a stormy May.

This too shall come to pass
When the dawn for once will cease to break
An autumn dews no longer make
A silver carpet of the slanting grass.

This too shall always be
When the world at last is freed from pain,
And men at last will see again
Their homeland in eternity.

UTOPIA

Find me a land where beauty never fades,
Where love is not a promise for tomorrow
Or yesterday's regret; find me a land
Where truth is reigning yet.

'Midst Alpine scenes I sought in vain
Or found it for an hour,
And lost again that mystic spell
Which darkened nights embower.

In ancient towns where art is bred
My soul was thrilled with joy,
But sadness whispered in my heart
'This beauty too shall die'.

When fair things fade and fair things die
I would that I had been
Born to a home beyong this earth
Where beauty rules as queen.

STORM

Through thunder's roar and lightning's flash
The colours shine serene,
The yellow of the primrose
And the landscape paved with green.

The silver of the beeches
And the knarled bark of oak
Seem listless when you see them
By the fir trees' constant cloak.

The gorse is blazing golden
Near the thickets on the hill
And in the shallow marshland
All life seems dead or still.

The lonely crane that stands aloof
Now flies on lazy wings
And from the heavens, black as pitch,
A murderous deluge springs.

The mountains in the distant blue
Soon vanish out of sight
And twilight, dusk and evening time
Put on their shroud of night.